"Every time people tell me they have decided to read the Bible straight through I put them on my prayer list, pretty sure their galoshes will fill with sand before they get halfway through the book of Joshua. Here, at last, is a better idea: enter the Bible through any of the fifty-two doors in this new abecedary by Anna Carter Florence, who will show you how much there is to gain from starting small and staying put with a few verses for a while. Whether her topic is an ax, a yak, or the queen of Sheba, she can sound as surprised as her reader to find how much is left to discover in a book we thought we already knew."

—**BARBARA BROWN TAYLOR**, author of *Always a Guest*
and *An Altar in the World*

"Anna Carter Florence has done it again—taken stories from the book that we love and breathed fresh wind into them and some of their lesser-known characters, objects, and even animals! As with much of Florence's writing, we fall in love. We fall in love with language, with biblical history, with imagination and wonder, and with the God who loves and delights in us. Florence takes the best stories and gives us her best stories. What a delightful gift for us that she continues to write."

—**ADRIENE THORNE**, Senior Minister,
The Riverside Church in the City of New York

"In *A Is for Alabaster,* Anna Carter Florence does what artists have always done: shows us how the art of language, story, character, plot, poetry, and shock can hold a mirror to the face of the reader and invite responses as strange and wondrous as the art. In response to a sculpture, Rilke said, 'You must change your life.' In response to the art of Scripture, Florence is a guide. She doesn't present these texts as safe—they're not—rather she praises their power."

—**PÁDRAIG Ó TUAMA**, author of *In the Shelter*

"I can think of no other person, scholar, teacher, or preacher whom I'd want to take me on a journey through the ABCs of Scripture. Anna Carter Florence is one of a kind! Her homiletical imagination will set you free. Read her words, and you will fall in love with the incarnate Word all over again."

—**LUKE A. POWERY**, Dean of the Chapel, Duke University,
and Professor of Homiletics, Duke Divinity School

"In this intriguing collection, it is fun to wander through the alphabet (twice!) with Anna Carter Florence. Her inventory from A to Z includes some old reliables, some fresh entries, and more than a few surprises. She brings to the interpretative task a rich background of study and the alert eye of a preacher. This rich recital of biblical data from A to Z is bound to illumine the reader and trigger many new insights into the text. It is a welcome, refreshing read."

—**WALTER BRUEGGEMANN**, William Marcellus McPheeters Professor Emeritus of Old Testament, Columbia Theological Seminary

"Whether you have been engaged in study of the Bible for a lifetime, are just beginning, or are anywhere in between, Anna Carter Florence's *A Is for Alabaster* will captivate you and create in you an insatiable desire for the Word. Her perspective of the ancient text makes it come alive and speak to its reader in fresh, powerful, and yet practical ways. This book will bless your life."

—**CYNTHIA L. HALE**, Senior Pastor, Ray of Hope Christian Church, Atlanta, Georgia

"With witticism and her signature wonder, Anna Carter Florence takes us on an alphabetical journey that will ignite inspiration and imagination in all who need and want to trust the Bible's truths. You will fall in love with Scripture all over again in ways you never imagined."

—**KAROLINE M. LEWIS**, Professor and the Marbury E. Anderson Chair of Biblical Preaching, Luther Seminary

"Everybody knows Anna Carter Florence, preacher and teacher of preachers, beloved for her creative, faithful, wise, and witty biblical interpretation. What a gift she has given us in *A Is for Alabaster*. Romping from Abigail to Zacchaeus, Anna offers a lively, often very funny, constantly insightful abecedary. What's an "abecedary"? In Anna Carter Florence's rendering, it's a playful but deeply theological celebration of the riches of Scripture, Old Testament and New. For us preachers, for those who love the Bible, for those who can't figure out how to read the Bible, but especially for those who may have fallen out of love with the Bible, what a gift!"

—**WILL WILLIMON**, Professor of the Practice of Christian Ministry, Duke Divinity School, and author of *God Turned toward Us*

"Whenever Anna Carter Florence and passages of Scripture are brought in close range, electricity arcs from one to the other, bringing insight and creativity. In these captivating and refreshing essays on biblical stories, she goes through the alphabet, A to Z, for the Old Testament and then again for the New Testament, and when she is finished, we are left both delighted and wishing that there were even more letters in the alphabet."

—**THOMAS G. LONG**, Bandy Professor Emeritus
of Preaching, Candler School of Theology

"I binged Anna Carter Florence's *A Is for Alabaster*. I told myself, "I have time for only one chapter," and then read five. I said, "I'll read a couple before falling asleep," and then read ten. I felt angry for Lot's wife, heartbroken for Naomi, and surprised by the queen of Sheba. I made plans to preach on Mary Magdalene, Nicodemus, and Onesiphorus. I was challenged by Quirinius and Rhoda. Readers will do more than enjoy Florence's imaginative retelling of Scripture. They will learn to read Scripture more joyfully. Florence makes the reader enthusiastic about the questions as she explores the world of Scripture with the thoughtfulness of a scholar and the creativity of a poet!!"

—**BRETT YOUNGER**, Senior Minister,
Plymouth Church, Brooklyn, New York

"In characteristic brisk and winsome style, Anna Carter Florence playfully explores the nether regions of the Bible, highlighting the forgotten (Puah, anybody?) centering the neglected (queen of Sheba), and relishing the obscure (Vashti). The result is like an offertory profession, bringing to the Lord's Table the full panoply of characters from the vast storehouse of Scripture. Florence embodies the householder in Jesus' parable who brings out of her treasure something old and something new: a chocolate box of delight."

—**SAM WELLS**, Vicar, St Martin in the Fields, London

"To preach Scripture, you have to love it, ingest it, digest it, and let it inhabit you. Only then can black-and-white print emerge as Technicolor in the retelling. No one does this better than Anna Carter Florence. She lets the texts deliver theology rather than theology usurp the text."

—**JOHN L. BELL**, The Iona Community, Scotland

IS FOR

Alabaster

A

IS FOR

Alabaster

52 REFLECTIONS

ON THE STORIES

OF SCRIPTURE

Anna Carter Florence

WJK WESTMINSTER
JOHN KNOX PRESS
LOUISVILLE • KENTUCKY

First edition
Published by Westminster John Knox Press
Louisville, Kentucky

23 24 25 26 27 28 29 30 31 32—10 9 8 7 6 5 4 3 2 1

Book design by Sharon Adams
Cover design by Leah Lococo

Library of Congress Cataloging-in-Publication Data

Names: Florence, Anna Carter, author.
Title: A is for alabaster : 52 reflections on the stories of scripture / Anna Carter Florence.
Description: First edition. | Louisville, Kentucky : Westminster John Knox Press, [2023] | Includes index. | Summary: "From the courageous Abigail to Zacchaeus in the sycamore tree, takes readers on an enchanting tour of the Old and New Testaments with reflections that reveal ancient wisdom and spark imagination anew"-- Provided by publisher.
Identifiers: LCCN 2023029713 (print) | LCCN 2023029714 (ebook) | ISBN 9780664261481 (paperback) | ISBN 9781646983445 (ebook)
Subjects: LCSH: Bible--Introductions. | Bible--Miscellanea.
Classification: LCC BS475.3 .F59 2023 (print) | LCC BS475.3 (ebook) | DDC 220.6/1--dc23/eng/20230731
LC record available at https://lccn.loc.gov/2023029713
LC ebook record available at https://lccn.loc.gov/2023029714

Most Westminster John Knox Press books are available at special quantity discounts when purchased in bulk by corporations, organizations, and special-interest groups. For more information, please e-mail SpecialSales@wjkbooks.com.

For David Carter Florence,
who fills my days with joy

Contents

Acknowledgments

*T*his book has been a long time in the making. The idea for it has been traveling with me since the day I read my parents' copy of Frederick Buechner's *Peculiar Treasures: A Biblical Who's Who* and was captivated by the writing as well as the book's A-to-Z structure.[1] I loved the freedom Buechner took to imagine these biblical characters. The writing was a marvel, as Buechner's always was. Someday, I thought, I'd like to do an ABC book like that—and so my first thanks must go to him, for the inspiration and example he set for me long ago. Frederick Buechner died on August 15, 2022, when I was in the last stages of writing this book. Like so many others, I am deeply grateful for the gift his life and work have been.

My next set of thanks goes to my students at Columbia Theological Seminary and to all the other students and preachers I've been privileged to meet and learn from over the years. This book was originally conceived as an alphabet for preachers—that is, reflections on the preaching life, drawn from biblical stories and images. It has evolved into something broader, with a wider audience in mind. I hope the book will be a welcoming one for any reader who picks it up. I also hope preachers will still hear a word in it for them, since echoes of the book's first focus (and my day job) may reverberate, from time to time.

1. The three books in Frederick Buechner's lexical trilogy are *Wishful Thinking: A Seeker's ABC* (1973), *Peculiar Treasures: A Biblical Who's Who* (1979), and *Whistling in the Dark: A Doubter's Dictionary* (1988).

I am grateful to my colleagues at Columbia, particularly Jacob D. Myers, my partner in all things homiletical. Jake offered encouragement at key moments, and it always helped. The Columbia Board approved my sabbatical leave, giving me time to write; President Victor Aloyo Jr. and Dean Christine Roy Yoder (and President Leanne Van Dyk and Dean Love Sechrest, before them) offered their generous support as well. Being part of the Columbia faculty and community for twenty-five years has been one of the great joys and privileges of my life, and I am thankful.

A vast network of friends and editors has sustained me through this project. Jessica Miller Kelley, my wonderful editor at Westminster John Knox Press, shepherded me through the final months and across a holiday finish line; David Maxwell, her predecessor, guided me through the proposal and early stages. My deep thanks to both, for believing in this book. Kathleen O'Connor, Geraldine Herbert, Karen Miller, Kim Long, Martha Moore-Keish, Karoline Lewis, Anna Stenund, Tina Johansson, Johan Svedberg, Carina Sundberg, and Christine Smith offered wisdom and encouragement along the way. My home congregation, Black Mountain Presbyterian Church, prayed for me and my writing every day during this last sabbatical, as did the Reverend Mary Katherine Robinson, our grace-filled pastor. I am so thankful for their love and support. And for friendship and constancy over many years and miles—not to mention the writing retreats in northern Iceland, and the weekly phone calls from Kópavogur—I thank Arnfríður Guðmundsdóttir, my sister of the heart. Someday we'll write a book together, and I'll learn to speak Icelandic.

And finally, for my beloved family, I don't have words big enough or deep enough to express the thanks and love I feel. I will simply record their names in my book of life: Gracie and Bill Florence, Lissy and Tim Rooney, Chris and Mary Carter, Caleb Florence, Jonah Florence, Kyra Harney, Jill Carter, and David Carter Florence. I thank my sister, Lissy, for her boundless love and brilliant travel companionship. I thank our sons, Caleb and Jonah, for being such an inspiration to their parents. I thank my mother, Jill Carter, for the hours and hours she spent with me on this project, patiently reading each new draft with her exquisite eye and ear for detail; her editing and enthusiasm have meant the world to me. And I thank my husband, David, for loving me through and cheering me on, and for years of careful listening to these biblical texts with me. His wisdom and insights always make mine better, and this book is the best example of that. For his joyful spirit, and the treasure he is in my life, I dedicate the book to him.

Introduction

I fell in love with Scripture the year I became a Sunday school dropout. It was the winter I was nine years old, and the saintly Mr. Moore was our fourth-grade Sunday school teacher. For the first time, we were actually reading from the Bible—a sturdy Revised Standard Version edition that had been presented to us at the end of third grade, with our names inscribed on the cover page—and it had been exciting to graduate from the glossy illustrated children's Bibles to this grown-up one with no pictures at all. Since September, we fourth-graders had dutifully sat around the long rectangular table with Mr. Moore at the head, while he led us in reading aloud from various passages. But it wasn't very interesting, and in my opinion we hadn't learned much at all beyond basic navigation around the Bible and how to pronounce some of the names.

I could tell Mr. Moore was deeply moved by the Scripture passages we read. His face lit up; this book was *alive* for him. But it wasn't for me, and I was frustrated. What, I wondered, was the trouble? Wasn't this supposed to be the year I was initiated into the mysteries of whatever these ancient words were saying? Wasn't I supposed to be as enthralled by them as the adults were? Why was fourth-grade Sunday school turning out to be so boring, and the Bible such a dull book to read?

After three months, I told my parents I'd had enough of the Bible and Sunday school, and I wasn't going back. It was the first time a book had ever disappointed me. It was the first time I'd ever rebelled, too, and my parents listened thoughtfully to my youthful indignation. "All right," they said. "Come up with an alternative for what you'll do with that hour, make a proposal, and we'll talk."

I did some fast thinking. My grandparents, savvy educators, had recently sent three gifts: the original cast recordings of *Godspell* and *Jesus Christ Superstar* and a book called *The Story Bible,* by Pearl S. Buck. The records, I'd already devoured, as they knew I would. The book, I had yet to read. So I proposed to read it each Sunday morning while the rest of my family was in Sunday school.

My parents agreed. And that's how I came to fall in love with Scripture as a nine-year-old religious rebel. Sunday mornings, when the other fourth-graders went obediently to class, I stayed behind in our parked car, under piles of blankets (New England winters are cold), reading *The Story Bible,* cover to cover. Each chapter had me riveted. No more dead words I couldn't pronounce. No more boring recitations. *The Story Bible* was just that—the Bible told as a longer narrative made up of dozens of smaller stories, each as thrilling as the other myths and folktales I adored: Aesop's fables and Grimm's fairy tales; Anansi and Coyote; and *D'Aulaires' Book of Greek Myths,* which I'd borrowed from the school library so many times that they finally gave me a copy.

Scripture came alive for me that winter. The stories leaped from the page with surprising energy, and I couldn't wait to follow: where would this one land today?! Where would that one lead?! The Bible was turning out to be the *least* dull book I'd ever read. And if I hadn't learned that in Mr. Moore's Sunday school class, I'd seen it in his face—for him, Scripture was a living story. *His* story. My story. I just needed to hear it in a form I recognized, with the freedom to imagine in my own voice.

Many decades later, I still find this to be true. Scripture speaks to me best when I give it more room—and give myself more room, too, to read with space and time and freedom. Sometimes that means leaving the structures of a particular classroom. Sometimes that means reading in unexpected and unusual places. Sometimes that means reading Bible stories alongside other stories and myths I love, so I remember Scripture is supposed to be (and is!) every bit as exciting. And sometimes that means reading like a nine-year-old Sunday school dropout who has had enough of *dead* and *boring* and knows that *a living story* is possible.

I hope that's some of what this book might be for you: a glimpse of how reading the Bible *could* be, and how *we* could be, with a little more room and freedom. The fifty-two reflections you'll find here—two for each letter of the English alphabet—are invitations for *you* to reflect and add your voice to this conversation. They aren't finished pieces. They won't provide definitive answers. But they might be starting points or trailheads or doorways to a place you've been wanting to explore.

The particular form the book takes is called an *abecedary*. An abecedary is a teaching tool: the alphabet written out as a primer, with each letter marking the beginning of a word or phrase. Students practiced their letters this way, as abecedaries in Middle English and Latin attest, and examples from the ancient world exist too. Hebrew abecedaries dating from 800 BCE and Ugaritic abecedaries from the thirteenth century BCE, carved in stone, were how scribes practiced their letter writing forms.[1] The book of Lamentations is an abecedary of sorts—an acrostic poem, each stanza beginning with a letter of the Hebrew alphabet.

Frederick Buechner's lexical trilogy—*Wishful Thinking: A Seeker's ABC* (1973), *Peculiar Treasures: A Biblical Who's Who* (1979), and *Whistling in the Dark: A Doubter's Dictionary* (1988)—makes use of the abecedary form, and so does this book, which was inspired by Buechner. Part of the enjoyment of writing it was picking the characters and images for each letter of the alphabet, but with only two rounds of A to Z to work with (and way too many characters whose names begin with *J*), I had to get creative to make room for everyone. Jacob, for instance, finds his place with "I is for Israel." Jonah takes "F is for Fish." Job is "W is for Whirlwind." And Jesus had to go rogue with a few incarnational verbs, like "G is for Growing Up" and

---

1. I thank my friend F. W. "Chip" Dobbs-Allsopp, professor of Old Testament and James Lenox Librarian at Princeton Theological Seminary, for these and other fun facts about ancient abecedaries, from his extensive knowledge of biblical and ancient Near Eastern literature and poetry. His latest book, *On Biblical Poetry* (New York: Oxford University Press, 2015), has been hailed as a seminal work in the field and the best of its kind in a generation.

"W is for Walking on Water," although he did claim the privilege of wandering in and out of everyone else's letters.

It has been a great adventure for me to commit to following these fifty-two stories up and down, around and about, and every other which way (since it would appear we never *did* take a direct route to wherever it was we were going). And reading Scripture is like that. It's more about the journey than the destination. Whether you're new to biblical literature or well seasoned and experienced in this regard, I hope you'll find encouragement here for your own reading journey—and even inspiration and a fresh take on some familiar stories, A to Z, if that's what you're looking for.

I believe this with all my heart: God is everywhere in the stories of Scripture, alive and moving in each one. And what if a way into these ancient mysteries was already ours to imagine?

It might be simpler and closer to home than we think.

Old Testament

A

IS FOR

ABIGAIL

1 Samuel 25

Then Abigail hurried and took two hundred loaves, two skins of wine, five sheep ready dressed, five measures of parched grain, one hundred clusters of raisins, and two hundred cakes of figs. She loaded them on donkeys and said to her young men, "Go on ahead of me; I am coming after you." But she did not tell her husband Nabal. As she rode on the donkey and came down under cover of the mountain, David and his men came down toward her, and she met them.

1 Sam. 25:18–20

*A*bigail must have known she wouldn't have an easy time of it when she married Nabal. The man's name means "Fool," and he was one. He was also rich and powerful and mean, with a surly disposition and a taste for raucous feasting and insulting other men. Nabal wasn't inclined to be generous or to give an inch of ground; when confronted, he was so ill-natured that no one could reason with him. Abigail, on the other hand, was the opposite of her husband. She was as clever and beautiful as he was stupid and loathsome. She knew how to work around him and, when necessary, clean up after him—skills she'd had plenty of chance to practice, as the wife of such a person.

It would be nice to report that Abigail's dreary life began to change the day her ogre of a husband was magically transformed into kindly Shrek with a heart of gold, but that's not quite how it went. Abigail's life began to change the day she learned that four hundred armed men were on the road to her house because her fool of a husband had just offended the biggest war hero in Israel.

7

The armed men were with David—the future King David—who was living through a rough patch, having recently been banished from court. David was the Lord's anointed, and King Saul had once embraced him like a son (see "G is for Goliath"). But Saul was unstable, plagued by jealousy and paranoia; his love for David turned to delusional accusations of treachery. For years, he'd been hunting David like a man possessed. David had fled to the wilderness and was living as an outlaw while he waited for the king's foul-weather mood to lift. His men were a band of merry misfits he'd attracted along the way ("Everyone who was in distress, and everyone who was in debt, and everyone who was discontented gathered to him" is how 1 Sam. 22:2 sums them up). As captain of this outfit, David wasn't exactly Robin Hood; he and his gang were running a protection racket among the local herdsmen. But his storied reputation preceded him, and people knew who he was. Abigail knew who he was. Her foolish husband, not so much.

It was shearing time, and Nabal had gone up to shear his three thousand sheep and one thousand goats. David heard of it and sensed that the rich man's herds might be his next business opportunity. He sent his men to position themselves as a wall around Nabal's flocks, shielding them from thieves while the shepherds worked. They hadn't been hired to provide this protection, but that was the racket: to show up and be a conspicuous presence, as courteous as they were intimidating to all concerned.

When the shearing was done, David's men went to Nabal and, in David's name, politely asked for payment: whatever food Nabal could spare for services rendered. It was generally understood that this request was more of a demand, and the herdsman would do well to cooperate. Nabal sneered in their faces. "Who is David?" he mocked. "Who is the son of Jesse? There are many servants today who are breaking away from their masters. Shall I take my bread and my water and the meat that I have butchered for my shearers and give it to men who come from I do not know where?" (vv. 10b–11).

David was furious. He immediately gave orders to four hundred of his men to strap on their swords and march with him to Nabal's house, to avenge the dishonor and disrespect the fool had shown. Why, he'd done this man a service, and Nabal had returned evil for good! David swore he'd make him pay in blood: "God do so to David and more also if by morning I leave so much as one male of all who belong to him" is how the New Revised Standard Version Updated Edition of the Bible reads, but what he really said was much cruder (see the footnote, if you want to know).[1]

David's temper was primed to explode. He may have shown restraint where King Saul was concerned—and had only just done so, in the chapter prior to this one, by refusing to kill Saul when he'd had the opening. But not with Nabal. The fool would get the full treatment, a battleground slaughter in his own backyard.

It might have come to that if Abigail hadn't intervened. One of Nabal's young men brought her the news of what her husband had done and what David was planning to do in return. With her entire household on the brink of disaster, Abigail didn't even bother trying to talk with Nabal. She left him to his cups and his table debauchery, and swiftly packed up all the food that should have been given to David's men in the first place. Then she loaded it all on donkeys, sent the gifts of food ahead, and followed on her own mount, to meet David and his men.

She had a plan, a speech, all ready. Abigail was a match for any war hero when it came to practical tactical brilliance.[2] She knew what was required when a man's ego and honor were injured, what to say to de-escalate tension and shift the focus away from the offender. She knew how to appease wounded pride, repair a chipped self-image, and appeal to a man's higher sense of self. And she knew that calling forth generosity, gratitude, and empathy were key to restoring honor and dignity. Somehow she found the words that turned David around and kept him from the stain of bloodguilt—vengeance that is not ours to take, that will forever haunt us if we do.

What Abigail said made a big impression on David. He blessed her for her words and sent her home in peace, with reassurances that four hundred men would not be marching on her house that day. She and

---

1. One translator puts it this way: "Thus may God do to David and even more, if I leave from all that is his until morning a single pisser against the wall!" Robert Alter, *The Hebrew Bible: A Translation with Commentary*, vol. 2, *Prophets* (New York: W. W. Norton, 2019), 282. Even the King James Version of the Bible doesn't hold back: "So and more also do God unto the enemies of David, if I leave of all that pertain to him by the morning light any that pisseth against the wall" (v. 22).

2. With thanks to Lin-Manuel Miranda and his *Hamilton* war heroes.

her household were safe, he said, because of her good sense. He didn't mention her courage, but we can: Abigail's courage was truly exceptional. If David had chosen to ignore her words (and she had no way of knowing whether he would or not), she might have been the first fatality of many. As it happened, the only fatality in Abigail's house was a death no one mourned: Nabal, who collapsed in shock when he heard what his wife had done. Abigail had waited until morning to tell him, when she was sure he'd be sober and would fully appreciate it—which we assume he did, because "his heart died within him; he became like a stone" (v. 37b). David declared it a fitting end to the fool who'd snubbed him, and promptly set about to woo the widow. Sharp-witted, eloquent Abigail became David's wife.

It would be nice to report that Abigail's words continued to make a big impression on David, that she was a wise and trusted counselor when he finally came to the throne. But that's not quite how it went. Abigail barely surfaces after the events in this chapter. She bears David a son named Chileab, who doesn't get much press or attention.[3] The boy is only one among David's many sons, the way Abigail is only one among David's many wives.

But Abigail's role in David's life has made a big impression in other places. She is remembered as a person who shaped David's moral character during a volatile and uncertain period of his life. She is regarded as a prophet for the way she called David out and back to his anointed role. She is the only woman in the Bible to be described as both intelligent and beautiful (in that order), and her speech is the longest by any woman in the Old Testament.[4]

Abigail has earned respect. A person does when she exercises unfailingly good judgment. And Abigail did, whether riding forth into danger or riding out years of foolishness; she beat outlaws and ogres with good sense alone. It's quite a record for a biblical character who is often among the last to be noticed. Unless we go alphabetically—and in that case, she leads.

---

3. See 2 Sam. 3:3.

4. L. Juliana Claassens, "An Abigail Optic: Agency, Resistance, and Discernment in 1 Samuel 25," in *Feminist Frameworks and the Bible: Power, Ambiguity, and Intersectionality,* ed. L. Juliana Claassens and Carolyn J. Sharp (London: Bloomsbury T&T Clark, 2017), 25.

B

IS FOR

BALAAM

Numbers 22

When the donkey saw the angel of the Lord, it lay down under Balaam, and Balaam's anger was kindled, and he struck the donkey with his staff. Then the Lord opened the mouth of the donkey, and it said to Balaam, "What have I done to you, that you have struck me these three times?" Balaam said to the donkey, "Because you have made a fool of me! I wish I had a sword in my hand! I would kill you right now!" But the donkey said to Balaam, "Am I not your donkey, which you have ridden all your life to this day? Have I been in the habit of treating you this way?" And he said, "No."

Then the LORD opened the eyes of Balaam, and he saw the angel of the LORD standing in the road, with his drawn sword in his hand, and he bowed down, falling on his face.

Num. 22:27–31

*T*he Bible has only two stories that feature animals who talk (to humans, that is), and if you had to guess, a snake and a donkey might not be the first you'd pick as most likely to start a conversation—which might be part of the fun here. What does a serpent want to discuss that your dog doesn't? When is a chipmunk most likely to interrupt? What *are* pressing matters for a donkey? These are intriguing questions. The thought of living in a world where animals, any animals, burst into speech at odd moments isn't odd at all for children who still inhabit fairy tales and Sesame Street, and perhaps it shouldn't be odd for adults either. In Scripture, animals are everywhere, and God has been known to give ravens, whales, and lions big roles at key junctures. In the book of Jonah, God even ordains a worm. Quite a few prophets wouldn't have survived without the creatures God sends to feed, save, or swallow them (or *not* swallow them, in the case of Daniel and those lions). And we know about the friendly beasts that kept baby Jesus company in the stable in Bethlehem—and then, apparently, sang songs about it.[1]

If God can call a worm as well as a prophet, or talk to a whale as easily as a human being (more easily, probably, given our track record), what would it be like to let go of an anthropocentric view of the universe to listen to *their* take on things? The animals in Scripture, talking or not, could be our summons to another world, and listening to their side of a story is a spiritual discipline many of us could benefit from. What does the lion say about the night Daniel was dropped into its den? How does the worm tell its call story? How does the whale talk about how it once had to reroute its migration pattern and swim hundreds of miles out of its way to swallow and then spit out a creature that tasted terrible and moaned the whole way? (See "F is for Fish.") St. Francis of Assisi would have been interested to hear. What's more, he would have asked, and suggested we do the same.

So would Balaam son of Beor. Balaam was a local seer, mystic, and medium-for-hire in Canaan when the Israelites were beginning their invasion of the land. The kings in the region were understandably concerned, and one of them, Balak son of Zippor, tried to enlist Balaam to put a curse on the invaders and their god. Balaam agreed to make contact with the Lord, and when he did, he was told to shut up and mind his own business: "The people are blessed," the Lord said. "Don't curse them, don't pursue this further, and don't you do or say a thing unless I tell you."

Balaam was used to being a middleman (between the earthly and spirit realms, that is), and perhaps he thought there might be a way to talk to all sides at once, in this particular triangle, and still get paid. He saddled up his donkey to ride to King Balak, not realizing that the

---

1. See 1 Kgs. 17:6 for the ravens, Jonah 1:17 for the whale—or "great fish," Dan. 6:22 for the lions, and Jonah 4:7 for the worm. "The Friendly Beasts," a traditional Christmas carol originating in medieval France, features a donkey, cow, sheep, and dove, each of whom takes a verse to describe a gift it gave the Christ child.

Lord had set an angel with a flaming sword in the middle of the road to block his way. But the donkey saw what was coming. Three times she tried to turn around, and each time Balaam beat the creature, growing more and more angry. Finally, the donkey gave up. "Have you lost your mind?!" she demanded. "Do you think I'd put on the brakes if I didn't have a good reason? Have I *ever* done anything like this, in all the years I've been carrying you?!" Balaam had to admit the donkey hadn't. And at that moment, God opened Balaam's eyes, and he saw what had been waiting for him: a murderous angel, sword in hand, who by then was hopping mad.

Balaam got an earful as the angel reamed him out. The only reason he was alive, the angel shouted, was because his donkey had seen what Balaam hadn't, and turned around. If it weren't for that, the angel would have slain Balaam right there and sent the donkey home without a scratch. So what did he think of that?!

Balaam apologized to all beings present and took the reprimand: *Don't you do or say a thing unless the Lord tells you.* If he and the donkey ever spoke again, we don't know. Perhaps they did. Or maybe Balaam just paid closer attention, now that he knew he lived in a world where animals, any animals, burst into speech at odd moments. Maybe he had a deeper sense of what it is to be a middleman listening for the spirit's voice amid a universe of wondrous, mysterious languages. Most of which we have yet to learn.

C

IS FOR

CALEB

Numbers 13

> The LORD said to Moses, "Send men to spy out the land of
> Canaan, which I am giving to the Israelites; from each of their
> ancestral tribes you shall send a man, every one a leader among
> them." . . .
>
> Moses sent them to spy out the land of Canaan and said to
> them, "Go up there into the Negeb, and go up into the hill coun-
> try, and see what the land is like and whether the people who
> live in it are strong or weak, whether they are few or many, and
> whether the land they live in is good or bad, and whether the
> towns that they live in are unwalled or fortified, and whether
> the land is rich or poor, and whether there are trees in it or not.
> Be bold, and bring some of the fruit of the land."
>
> Num. 13:1–2, 17–20

*I*srael conducted two reconnaissance missions to the land of Canaan
to spy on its inhabitants, and Caleb was one of the twelve men who
took part in the first. (The second—see "R is for Rahab"—didn't
happen for another forty years and gets a more sinister telling in the
book of Joshua. It's like a very dark season 2 of a miniseries.) When
the first one took place, only two years had passed since the Israelites'
miraculous escape from slavery in Egypt. They had been wandering
in the wilderness of Sinai and were poised to enter the land God had
promised to give them—but they knew nothing about it. They didn't
know if it was good land or barren, fertile or arid, or whether the
people who lived in it were likely to welcome six hundred thousand
new neighbors. They didn't know if they had a fight on their hands or

whether the fight was even worth winning. Moses, on God's orders, picked one leader from each of the twelve tribes to sneak over the hills, scout out the environs, and bring back word on what lay in store. Caleb was the representative from the tribe of Judah.

The mission took forty days, and the men came back with figs and pomegranates and a cluster of grapes. The land, as they had learned, was indeed a good one—exceedingly good, as Caleb exclaimed. It was flowing with milk and honey, just as the Lord had said. It surpassed everything they could have hoped for in a new home. And it was worth fighting for, if the Lord was with them—which Caleb asserted was completely the case.

The other eleven spies weren't as convinced as Caleb was. The land was good, yes, but the people were strong and their cities well fortified. This was not a fight the Israelites could hope to win. Better not to engage, the eleven advised Moses. Caleb tried to calm their fears with assurances of the power of God, but the eleven were on a roll. They resorted to inciting mass hysteria, something the Israelites were already well practiced in. "The land is terrible!" the eleven cried. "The people are giants! To them, we are grasshoppers! We'll all be devoured!" And right on schedule, the wail arose: "Why did we ever leave Egypt? Let's choose a commander and go back!"

This was not the first time Moses had heard such moaning and groaning, and it wouldn't be the last. But it had to be one of the most deflating. To be so close—on the cusp of the promised land! And to have such a fine report of that land, from a trusted leader like Caleb! Why was fear always the people's worst enemy? Why did it dupe them, over and over again, into thinking that a bondage they knew was preferable to a liberation they might live?

One voice against eleven, one voice shouting in the wilderness, might seem like terrible odds. But Caleb had a different spirit.[1] He believed in the promises of God: the glory of the Lord would be revealed. If the Israelites went up into this land, they would overcome whatever barriers lay between it and them—and the biggest of those was their own fear. "We can overcome that too," Caleb tried to assure the people, looking around at the whole assembly.

1. See Num. 14:20–27.

One voice against eleven, one voice shouting in the wilderness, one voice trying to allay the fears of six hundred thousand, is what life and faith can feel like sometimes. When we find ourselves in rough country with no clear way through, anxiety and fear can turn backwoods into wasteland. We know a wasteland is no place to live, no place that will sustain life. The call, then, is to search for the places that *will* sustain life, growth, healing, hope. So here is the call: Scout out the territory beyond our present wilderness. Bring back a report of what could be, if we're brave enough to believe it. Encourage the ones with us to move forward, with God's help. Remind them of the promises of God. Refuse to accept the false reports of those who say this land, these foes, this wound, this fight, is too much for us; it is impossible. Hold fast to a different spirit—one of hope, not fear.

It might seem a bit dramatic to think of that work as a recon mission. But there is a stealth and canniness and cunning to the call to live into God's vision, the one that lies over these hills and beyond this wilderness where the people of God keep getting bogged down. Sometimes we have to scope out a strategy our companions are terrified to try. Sometimes one voice is the only true and truthful one, trying to get a hearing among eleven other false (and hysterical) reports.

Caleb did manage to persuade one of his fellow spies, in the end: Joshua, from the tribe of Ephraim. The two of them pleaded with the Israelites to remain steadfast, in vain, as it turned out. The Israelites were too hyped up and too far gone, which can happen in the community of faith, and in cities and nations too. The result was an extension of their wilderness time—forty years' worth, one for every day the spies spent in Canaan—and God's firm promise that none of those who had joined the panic would ever set foot in the promised land. As for the ten remaining spies, the ones who gave false testimony to provoke a frenzy, God had a rejoinder for them as well: a plague smackdown. They were gone in no time. And the voice that remained, the one that endured, was Caleb's.

This isn't a story that sits well with modern readers—marauding Israelites, preparing to steal land and slaughter Canaanites in their way—and we have good reason to be cautious: "God's promised land . . . for *us*" has been a rallying cry and justification for many of civilization's worst atrocities. These particular biblical accounts are ones we must read and probe carefully.

But the story of Caleb, speaking truth into a whirlwind of lies, is one we *can* enter for a moment. We know that script well. And we know the eleven other voices—which is why we need Caleb's skill as a scout, his calm in a storm, and a portion of his different spirit.

D

IS FOR

DELIVERANCE

Exodus 2

Now a man from the house of Levi went and married a Levite woman. The woman conceived and bore a son, and when she saw that he was a fine baby, she hid him three months. When she could hide him no longer she got a papyrus basket for him and plastered it with bitumen and pitch; she put the child in it and placed it among the reeds on the bank of the river. His sister stood at a distance, to see what would happen to him.

The daughter of Pharaoh came down to bathe at the river, while her attendants walked beside the river. She saw the basket among the reeds and sent her maid to bring it. When she opened it, she saw the child. He was crying, and she took pity on him. "This must be one of the Hebrews' children," she said. Then his sister said to Pharaoh's daughter, "Shall I go and get you a nurse from the Hebrew women to nurse the child for you?" Pharaoh's daughter said to her, "Yes." So the girl went and called the child's mother. Pharaoh's daughter said to her, "Take this child and nurse it for me, and I will give you your wages." So the woman took the child and nursed it. When the child grew up, she brought him to Pharaoh's daughter, and he became her son. She named him Moses, "because," she said, "I drew him out of the water."

Exod. 2:1–10

*W*hat a perfect story.

Pharaoh makes chaos, mother makes ark.
Princess finds baby, sister brokers deal.
Baby saved, Pharaoh foiled.

A perfect story, with great roles for girls, we might add (not quite "The Bible Meets *Frozen,*" but almost). Right off the top, we notice two things. The first is that the main characters are young people, and *their parents aren't around.* That's important, because this is a story about what happens when the young people are in charge. The second is that without this story, without these two girls, there is no Moses. There is no exodus. There is no deliverance for the children of Israel—and there won't be, unless the parents get off the stage and the young people set things in motion.

So we have our two stock roles for girls, here: beautiful princess and responsible big sister. They're both good parts, better written than the ones we usually see, with more substance too. We can be Pharaoh's daughter, clad in silks, dipping our lovely toes in the cool green water, or we can be Moses' sister, alone in the reeds, keeping watch over our basket by day and by night. Whichever part we pick, we can't lose; they're both strong characters, smart and resourceful. And while the story doesn't tell us exactly how old they were, whether they were twenty-somethings or teenagers or even younger, what it does tell us is that each of them had an inner rebel just waiting to be unleashed. Each of them was ready to set aside what she *should* do and work together on what they *might* do—which can happen when we're down in the reeds.

The story's setting is Egypt, a superpower in those days, where the Hebrews are the Egyptians' slaves. But the Hebrew population is growing. It's big enough to make Pharaoh, the king of Egypt, feel threatened that soon these people will be almost as numerous as his own: he'll go downtown and hear Hebrew spoken as much as he hears Egyptian—which for him is darkly worrisome. To address the situation, he comes up with an unspeakably evil and effective plan to control the Hebrews. He targets their boys. Every Hebrew baby boy that is born, Pharaoh orders his Egyptian citizens, is to be exterminated on sight; pitch them in the Nile. Pharaoh knows: Destroy the boys, and eventually he will break and destroy the people (see "P is for Puah").

Little Moses is a boy, and when he is born, his mother does what she can to hide him for a while. But babies grow. And when she can hide him no longer, Moses' mother takes a bunch of papyrus, loams it with the ancient equivalent of Kevlar, and makes a snug little ark for her three-month-old son. It's a brilliant act, a symbolic act, designed to save life as well as to bear witness. It's also heartbreakingly limited. A Kevlar ark can't save a child for long. He has one day, maybe two, before he will die of exposure; one day, maybe two, to live. Yet anyone who finds him will get the mother's message, loud and clear:

> This is what we've come to, in Egypt.
> Take a look: Kevlar cradles.
> It's all I could do for my child.
> All I could give him was two more days.

With that, the mother leaves the scene. Maybe she was like Hagar, who couldn't bear to watch baby Ishmael die in the desert, in Genesis 21; we don't know. But we do know it's the sister who takes over from here. That's what big sisters do: they watch when the parents leave and report back. It's their job, as part of the family, and it was *this* sister's job. She was to stand at a distance and see what happened to her baby brother.

Pharaoh's daughter enters the scene next. She has a different agenda. She comes down to the river to take a bath and get away from it all—the court, the publicity, the pressure, the pedestal. Being beautiful is a tough job. But that's what princesses are: everything we dream we could be. It's their job, as part of the family, and it was *this* princess's job. She was to take her maids, go to the river, and anoint her lovely skin so she'd look good for the paparazzi that afternoon.

Here they are, then—two girls in the reeds who know exactly what their jobs are. *Hide and watch. Bathe and dress. Do as you're told and come home.* And they might have done it and never met one another, but the reeds are a watery, slippery, in-between sort of place. It's muddy there, and murky, and hard to find footing, and who knows where the deep water starts? Anything can happen down in the reeds to upset a girl's balance, and on this day, something did.

We know what it was. The princess found the baby. The *Egyptian* princess found the *Hebrew* baby—and we know what she was supposed to do with it. So did she. So did the sister. And *now* what? What do you do with a baby in a basket when you're down in the reeds, at the river's edge, and the parents, *your* parents, are not around?

The princess knew what her father would do, or at least what his law decreed. If this was a Hebrew male child (and it was), she was supposed to tip over the basket and let that baby tumble into the water. At the very least, she should close the lid, give the little ark a push, and send it on down the river for someone else to deal with. That's what the law required, like it or not, and she was supposed to uphold it.

The sister knew what her mother would want her to do. If someone found the baby, even if that someone was an Egyptian, the sister was supposed to keep watching, as awful as things might get. She was to stay in her hiding place and keep quiet, so she wasn't seen and she wasn't caught, and then report to her mother all that had happened. That's what times like these required, like it or not, and she was supposed to just try and survive.

Two girls in the reeds, with a little body between them. They knew what their parents wanted them to do—*but they didn't do it.* They couldn't. Things look different when we're down in the reeds; we have to think for ourselves and tell it like we see it. And that's what the princess did. "This," she said, "must be one of the Hebrews' children."

Sometimes the most radical thing a person can say is the truth, just naming what we see right in front of us. That baby left to die in a basket. That child washed up on the beach. That boy's body left for hours in the street. Just telling the truth about it is huge—saying it out loud, and letting it reverberate in the air. *This must be one of the Hebrews' children, because no other mothers are reduced to making little arks to float in the Nile, trying to save their babies from a flood of hate.*

One truth calls forth another, especially when we're down in the reeds. One girl, stammering out the truth about what she sees, empowers another girl to speak up too. One girl, pausing over unspeakable evil, encourages another girl to stand with her. "This must be one of the Hebrews' children," said the princess, and then the sister got an idea. "Do you want me to find a nurse among the Hebrew women?" she asked, stepping out from her hiding place. "Do you want me to find someone to nurse that child—for *you*?"

And just like that, they had a plan. A plan to save one life, no matter what their parents thought of it. And it was about the craziest plan you could think of, to take baby Moses back to his Hebrew mother for a few years and tell everyone it was *just fine* because it was on Pharaoh's daughter's orders. But they did it, and they got away with it, and when Moses was three years old, the princess adopted him. She took him into the palace and raised him there, with her father down the hall, and God only knows what *he* thought about this whole arrangement—little Moses sitting in his booster seat at the royal table and riding his Little Tikes chariot through the throne room—Scripture never says a word about *that*. But then, this isn't a story about the parents and doing what they told you, even if your dad is the pharaoh. This is a story about the young people doing whatever crazy things they can dream up together to get the bodies out of the reeds.

Did they know what they were setting in motion? If they didn't, we do. God's liberating work starts down in the reeds, with an interruption we didn't expect and a body we must acknowledge. God's deliverance of a people can start with two girls and one really wild idea. That's it; that's all we need. Because whenever the children of God claim the freedom to re-imagine and remix the world, it's a *double* deliverance: Moses can grow up. The exodus can begin—and we all need to leave Egypt. It's the next chapter of a perfect story, maybe one we'll write.

E

IS FOR

ESTHER

Esther 4

Then Esther spoke to Hathach and gave him a message for Mordecai: "All the king's servants and the people of the king's provinces know that, if any man or woman goes to the king inside the inner court without being called, there is but one law: to be put to death. Only if the king holds out the golden scepter to someone may that person live. I myself have not been called to come in to the king for thirty days." When they told Mordecai what Esther had said, Mordecai told them to reply to Esther, "Do not think that in the king's palace you will escape any more than all the other Jews. For if you keep silent at this time, relief and deliverance will rise for the Jews from another place, but you and your father's family will perish. Who knows? Perhaps you have come to royal dignity for just such a time as this." Then Esther said in reply to Mordecai, "Go, gather all the Jews to be found in Susa, and hold a fast on my behalf, and neither eat nor drink for three days, night or day. I and my maids will also fast as you do. After that I will go to the king, though it is against the law, and if I perish, I perish."

Esth. 4:10–16

*E*sther shows up only once in the Revised Common Lectionary, in Year B, the nineteenth Sunday after Pentecost, Proper 21 (26). Perhaps that's commentary in itself: maybe the opportunities for us to step up and lean into a great act of courage come around so seldom that we get only one or two over the span of a lifetime. Maybe those moments of courage turn out to make a difference for hundreds or even thousands of people. Maybe, for that reason, they're remembered

23

as great acts of heroism, even if it's not what we intended. In which case the issue seems to be: Will we recognize a singular moment and seize it when it comes? Will we find the courage to step into a void with no guaranteed outcome? Or will we hesitate just long enough for the moment to pass by, beyond recall?

How do we live in such a way that courage is available to us when we need it?

There are no formulas, as Esther's story so aptly illustrates. She never asked for heroism. She never asked to be born in an empire hostile to her Jewish faith. She never asked to lose her parents and be raised by her uncle Mordecai, no matter how kind and wise he was. She never asked to be selected as a replacement queen in a kingdom-wide search meant as a royal distraction, after the former queen's courage ended up publicly embarrassing the king (see "V is for Vashti"). And she never asked for Haman, the king's hell-bent-on-revenge adviser, to manipulate the monarch into signing an edict to destroy all the Jews in the empire, simply because his ego was threatened by one man who refused to bow to him. Esther's uncle Mordecai bowed to no one but the Lord of the Universe, and Haman, who felt entitled to Mordecai's deference and subjugation, was enraged by it. So Haman conceived a plan that played into public xenophobia and nationalism: because Mordecai dared to stand, all Jews would pay the price. They would *all* be annihilated. Esther never asked for that. And she certainly never asked to be trapped in the middle of an insane power struggle for male dominance in the court—a struggle that, because of one man's rage, quickly ramped up to full-blown genocide.

From the confines of the harem, Esther felt deflated and defeated enough to go down into silence: What could one woman in her position possibly do to stop an imperial juggernaut? Why should she think they would ever listen to her?

Mordecai suggested she reframe the issue:

> Do not think that in the king's palace you will escape any more than all the other Jews. For if you keep silent at this time, relief and deliverance will rise for the Jews from another place, but you and your father's family will perish.

Who knows? Perhaps you have come to royal dignity for just such a time as this. (vv. 13b–14).

The issue isn't whether we have enough power to confront injustice. It's whether we recognize that it's time to step up and try. Time to speak. Time to act. Time to use whatever we have at our disposal, even if it's a set of royal robes and a tiara. Or jeans and a T-shirt: those could work.

Esther recognized her moment when it came around. Even more amazing, she seized it. And because of that, we remember her as one of the greatest heroines of her time and ours, a woman who stepped out of obscurity and hiding (which is what her name means; Esther literally means "I am hiding") into a blazing spotlight of uncertain outcomes. There were no guarantees that she would succeed. There were no guarantees that she would survive. There was simply the imperative of the moment, and the truth, and the hope that her voice would be heard. Maybe she *was* sent to the kingdom for such a time as that. Maybe she *did* have enough courage to take a deep breath and use what she had.

Esther doesn't surface much in Christian lectionary cycles. But our Jewish sisters and brothers have the right idea: Read the whole book, out loud and in worship. Do it every year, as the biblical text prescribes. Make it a festival called Purim, to commemorate the story. Get the children involved, with costumes and parades. Raise them with the expectation that the story of Esther isn't optional or occasional; it's written into our life. It's written into our faith. And it will come up each year, and then again in each life, and we have all that we need to play it.

F

IS FOR

FISH

Jonah 1

Now the word of the LORD came to Jonah son of Amittai, saying, "Go at once to Nineveh, that great city, and cry out against it, for their wickedness has come up before me." But Jonah set out to flee to Tarshish from the presence of the LORD. He went down to Joppa and found a ship going to Tarshish; so he paid his fare and went on board, to go with them to Tarshish, away from the presence of the LORD.

But the LORD hurled a great wind upon the sea, and such a mighty storm came upon the sea that the ship threatened to break up. Then the sailors were afraid, and each cried to his god. They threw the cargo that was in the ship into the sea, to lighten it for them. Jonah, meanwhile, had gone down into the hold of the ship and had lain down and was fast asleep. . . .

Then [the sailors] said to him, "What shall we do to you, that the sea may quiet down for us?" For the sea was growing more and more tempestuous. He said to them, "Pick me up and throw me into the sea; then the sea will quiet down for you, for I know it is because of me that this great storm has come upon you." Nevertheless, the men rowed hard to bring the ship back to land, but they could not, for the sea grew more and more stormy against them. Then they cried out to the LORD, "Please, O LORD, we pray, do not let us perish on account of this man's life. Do not make us guilty of innocent blood, for you, O LORD, have done as it pleased you." So they picked Jonah up and threw him into the sea, and the sea ceased from its raging. Then the men feared the LORD even more, and they offered a sacrifice to the LORD and made vows.

But the LORD provided a large fish to swallow up Jonah, and Jonah was in the belly of the fish three days and three nights.

Jonah 1:1–5, 11–17

*J*onah never wanted to be a prophet. That, in itself, isn't a bad thing. As the saying goes, "Never trust a prophet who signs up for the job." On the other hand, when God calls, it's time to *go. Now.* Prophets who have been summoned are expected to step up and do the job, promptly. This is where Jonah gets into trouble. He goes when he's summoned, but not to Nineveh, the city God has in mind. He goes in the opposite direction and buys a ticket to sail to the city of Tarshish, which in Jonah's day was the ends of the earth.[1] It was the farthest a person could go before the world dropped off. Jonah bets this will be far enough to run from both God and Nineveh.

It isn't. God chases him down to the coast and all the way out to sea. When Jonah still refuses to pay attention, God sends gale-force winds and a storm so big, even the ship has a nervous breakdown (as the Hebrew puts it).[2] This is God's way of demonstrating that Jonah's prophetic assignment is not, in fact, optional. He can try to hide below deck, or at world's end in Tarshish, but it will be a fruitless enterprise. God wants *him.* In Nineveh. To speak the word God will give him. Jonah finally realizes that he can hide no longer and has put others in danger, since the storm is clearly designed for him. He tells the crew to toss him overboard so the winds and waves will cease. The crew does, reluctantly, and the storm stops, abruptly. Jonah is in the water, not even bothering to swim. He expects that this is it: he's about to drown at sea. He figures that's what you get when you refuse to obey the call of God.

It isn't. What you get is a big fish with a directive to swallow up. *You,* that is—by which we mean *us.*

To be swallowed up is not the friendliest of human experiences. It comes to each of us, eventually, but through less tangible agents than sea creatures. Anxiety and guilt. Anger and fear. Sorrow and pain. Each of those is capable of swallowing us up and then carrying us long distances in the cold and the wet, to places we never wanted to go. Places where God feels as far away as Tarshish, or even Sheol, the pit—as they called it in Jonah's day.

---

1. Tarshish was on the Iberian Peninsula, in present-day Spain.

2. See Yvonne Sherwood, *A Biblical Text and Its Afterlives: The Survival of Jonah in Western Culture* (New York: Cambridge University Press, 2000), 250–51.

But to be swallowed up by a big fish, Jonah-style, is different. To begin with, the fish is a saving device. Without it, we'd be lost to the waves and dead in the water. As surely as day follows night, a big fish like Jonah's is a life raft sent from God. It just happens to be more pointedly metaphorical: cramped, slippery, and filled with fish guts. We won't be able to move, stand, or see the hand in front of our face, and we won't be able to steer or navigate either. This is the whole point: we're not supposed to be in control. We're supposed to get a taste of what an aquatic netherworld is like. The big fish is the perfect holding pen for any of us who may be pretending we can't hear what God is calling us to say or do. In God's estimation, we may need some time to think about that—three days, in Jonah's case— before something far worse can drag us down and swallow us whole.

Since the big fish is only a temporary shelter, there needs to be an exit strategy. So God sends the fish a new directive, as soon as a little dry land becomes available. After the swallow-up directive comes another one: spew out. *You,* that is—by which we mean *us.*

Notice that we aren't cast back into the waves to drown, but we don't exactly get a hero's welcome on the beach either. The fish spews us out. It hurls us back into our lives. There's nothing grace-ful about this, as anyone who has suffered a bout of seasickness or stomach flu knows. It's regurgitation with fish guts. It's salvation by projectile vomiting. It might even be resurrection with a whole lot of slime. There's nothing to do but go with it. Let the eruption happen. And then, be a grown-up. Do what needs to be done. Pick up our pride, wash off the mess, and thank God for another chance to go to Nineveh—where no one really wants to go, but where we're all sent, at some point. After sitting a spell in the big fish, if that's required.

Swallowed up, spewed out. Is it any wonder that so many of us over the years have identified with Jonah? It isn't his initial running away that hits home with us, although most of us have tried it. It's that his actions are so laughably ineffectual. We can't run away from God's call to speak any more than we can hide in fig leaves. We can't set sail for Tarshish any more than we can walk to Mars. And we can't hide below deck in a storm when there's work to do and a word to say. God will send a big fish to find us—as often as necessary. And in this story, it's the fish that takes us where we need to go. It's the fish that saves us from a far worse fate, so we can be the person God has called us to be.

Swallowed up, spewed out. The next time we find ourselves on the receiving end of one of those verbs, we might ask ourselves if a big fish is involved. Maybe this experience of feeling overwhelmed or engulfed by some emotion *isn't* what we think it is. Could God have a word for us to speak in Nineveh, a word that we're taking a little too long to say? Have we somehow fallen asleep below deck in a storm?

We'll need to feel around with our feet, to check. If those are fish guts slopping under our shoes, chances are we're on our way to the beach in the belly of a fish, and it's for our own good. Best not to fight it. Hunker down and use the time to sort out priorities. Pray like Jonah, sing like Jonah, and prepare for a wet landing.

G

IS FOR

GOLIATH

1 Samuel 17

Saul clothed David with his armor; he put a bronze helmet on his head and clothed him with a coat of mail. David strapped Saul's sword over the armor, and he tried in vain to walk, for he was not used to them. Then David said to Saul, "I cannot walk with these, for I am not used to them." So David removed them. Then he took his staff in his hand and chose five smooth stones from the wadi and put them in his shepherd's bag, in the pouch; his sling was in his hand, and he drew near to the Philistine.

1 Sam. 17:38–40

*G*oliath of Gath was the Philistine giant that no one in Israel wanted to fight, and for good reason. The man was a behemoth: he stood nearly ten feet tall, his whole body was covered with bronze, and he carried a spear as big as a tree. He also liked to yell a lot. He came out to the battlefield every day and yelled at the Israelite army to send him one of their own to fight, so they could settle this long dispute between the Philistines and King Saul once and for all, but there were never any takers; the Israelites were terrified of him. It was a matter of national shame, and it went on for forty days. Goliath would come out morning and evening and shout his defiance, and the Israelite army would turn and run. In desperation, Saul finally offered his own daughter and a treasure chest of riches to the man who'd agree to fight the Philistine champion and kill him, but still no one came forward to try.

Intimidation, as every bully knows, is a powerful instrument. If you can make all those around you believe that they don't have what it takes to stand up to you, you can defeat an army just by yelling at it. You can also depress a person who is facing the prospect of speaking a word of truth in this world.

We know Goliath well. He shows up regularly at our homes and workplaces and faith communities, and he stamps his foot and shakes his spear and yells at us. Sometimes he shows up twice a day, morning and evening; when he can, he sets up camp in our heads. He bellows about everything: how small we are, how green we are, how unfit for life and work in the real world. He hollers about the ridiculousness of whatever work or ministry we do, in whatever capacity. Mostly, though, he tries to turn our attention from Scripture to him. If he can get us to fight back using weapons, rather than the Word of God, he knows he'll have us. If he can provoke us into returning violence for violence, our words will be as empty as he says they are.

Goliath is a gear in the machinery of the powers and principalities, and he has to be defeated. But not on his own terms. Not with his own swords and spears. With the Word, which is all any of us has to fight with in the end: the liberating, life-giving, soul-saving, body-redeeming Word of God.[1] We meet it in Scripture, and with God's help, we speak it. When justice comes on this earth, when the oppressed go free, it will not be with Goliath's weapons. It will be with the Word, sharper and stronger than any sword, with *proclamation* in all its forms.

If Goliath is a given, then how do we deal with all the noise he makes? How do we stand up to him with faith and confidence in what the Word of God can do, without losing nerve and heart?

This story has two suggestions for us. Don't try to be what you aren't, and don't get too caught up in the snares and fears of adulthood. Recognize that there are moments—and your daily face-off with Goliath is one of them—when it helps to be in touch with your inner adolescent.

We need to take a brief excursus into social and developmental theory here. Adolescents have acute sensibility factors when it comes

---

1. Charles L. Campbell, professor emeritus of homiletics at Duke Divinity School, has written extensively on this, and the terminology is his. See *The Word before the Powers: An Ethic of Preaching* (Louisville, KY: Westminster John Knox Press, 2002).

to bullies; they have daily experience in the subject. They know what Goliath looks and sounds and smells like. They know how close they can get to him before he roars, and they know how far they can push. They're also developmentally programmed to overestimate their own strength in all things, which makes them (1) vulnerable, (2) irrepressible, and (3) invincible. Is it any wonder that justice movements the world over rely on youth to fuel their revolutions? Adults may quail, but an adolescent at the peak of her idealism will believe herself fit for the task of slaying a giant. A teenager who weighs less than Goliath's *armor* will dare to take him on. It's the gift of the age, and it's one that adults would do well to reclaim when courage fails.

The particular teenager who volunteers to be a giant-killer in this story is young David, fresh from the sheep pasture, where he's been consigned to look after the flocks and stay out of trouble. Or so his family thinks. Actually, shepherding is a dangerous business, and David's been learning all kinds of survival skills with a slingshot. His older brothers may be in the army, but David does battle of his own against the predators of this world who threaten God's flocks. To hear him tell it (and he does), he can rescue a lamb from the mouth of a bear. He can grab a lion by its jaw and kill it with his bare hands. And he is shocked to learn that no one in Saul's army has stepped up to meet Goliath. What's this Philistine, after all, but an oversized bear with a shield in its paw? And why does no one in Israel trust that God will deliver them with a mighty Word?

David assures Saul that despite his youth and inexperience, he's nonetheless fully capable of dealing with Goliath. How can it be otherwise, he asks, if God is with him? The boy is as buoyant as Saul is grim. None of the adults in the story expect David to survive, but that is *their* age-related challenge: adults are developmentally programmed to be drearily realistic. To underscore this, Saul outfits David for battle with state-of-the-art technology, the way one does in the real world. But you can't dismantle a giant with his own tools, no matter how advanced those tools are.

The outcome is all but obvious, if we're acquainted with heroic sagas, comic books, or teenage chutzpah. David fells Goliath with one well-aimed stone, which no one believed would be possible, and he does it without the trappings of grown-up warfare. He won't wear armor that isn't his. He won't carry weapons he doesn't know. He simply goes to meet the giant with the familiar things he relies on every day: some stones, a slingshot, and the Word of God. Sometimes the humblest, most basic things are all we need to shut up a very loud giant.

Whenever we are intimidated by the bullies on the block—the ones that tell us we aren't strong enough, smart enough, brave enough, or technologically savvy enough to do what God has called us to do—we need to reread this story. If we believe Goliath, he'll always win. If we put on armor that isn't ours, we won't get far. The way to fell a giant is with a well-placed word of truth: the Word set loose. So channel your inner adolescent, reacquaint yourself with obstinate idealism, and tell that giant his days are numbered.

H

IS FOR

HABAKKUK

Habakkuk 2

> I will stand at my watchpost
>   and station myself on the rampart;
> I will keep watch to see what he will say to me
>   and what he will answer concerning my complaint.
> Then the LORD answered me and said:
> Write the vision;
>   make it plain on tablets,
>   so that a runner may read it.
> For there is still a vision for the appointed time;
>   it speaks of the end and does not lie.
> If it seems to tarry, wait for it;
>   it will surely come; it will not delay.
>
> Hab. 2:1–3

*H*abakkuk is the eighth of the twelve Minor Prophets of the Hebrew Bible. Little is known for certain about this prophet or the time and setting of his words, except that he is presented as a witness to invasions of Jerusalem. The short book that bears his name is only three chapters long. Unless you go hunting for it, you might miss it completely. If his name intimidates you, you might skip it on purpose—but don't. To miss Habakkuk is to miss a preacher's heart and one of Scripture's most powerful interpretations of the call to speak.

Habakkuk has an urgent message of hope for the people, but he also has an urgent question. When the times are dire and the backdrop is war, where will you stand to bring a vision of hope? What will your pulpit be, and what will that pulpit look like?

Pulpits come in all sorts of shapes. We can find pulpits that are open or closed, winged or tiered, square or round, columned or boxed. They might be imposing structures, located front and center, or simple lecterns off to one side. They might be carved to look like desks or wineglasses or baptismal tubs or a ship's prow. In an Anglican church, we might see an eagle-shaped lectern. One Egyptian Revival-style church has a pulpit in the form of a phoenix.[1] Each of these designs speaks volumes about the theologies of preaching that formed these communities and may guide them still. A pulpit shaped like an eagle is clearly communicating something ("preaching is soaring on strong winds of the Spirit"); so is a pulpit shaped like a phoenix ("preaching is calling forth new life from the ashes"). A desk-shaped pulpit refers to the preacher's vocation as a scholar. A wineglass-shaped pulpit points to the sacramental nature of proclamation.

But a rampart-shaped pulpit? That's something we likely haven't seen. Unless we've been reading the prophet Habakkuk, in which case we know that sometimes ramparts are all a preacher has to stand on.

For Habakkuk, preaching is keeping watch from the battlements while a war rages. His pulpit is no desk or wineglass; it's a rampart. It has crenellated walls and stone castle strength. It has covered parapets and built-in watchtowers. It looks like an oversized chess piece just dropped into the front of the church. Zoom in, and we can see the preacher pacing the walls, peering into the distance. Lean in, and we can hear the preacher pounding fists against stone, shouting up at the sky: *I'll stand at my watchpost and station myself on the rampart! I'll keep watch to see what God will say to me and what the Lord will answer me concerning my complaint!*

The rampart-shaped pulpit is for times of warfare, not internal squabbles within the community or petty complaints lobbed in the preacher's direction. *Real* warfare, the kind that goes beyond turf battles and interpretive skirmishes. The rampart-shaped pulpit is an unequivocal reminder that the context for our proclamation is

---

1. Downtown Presbyterian Church in Nashville is an Egyptian Revival-style building designed by architect William Strickland in the mid-nineteenth century.

perilous and life-threatening, because an enemy has invaded our city, an enemy that means to lay siege and destroy us.

For Habakkuk, that enemy was an army at the city gates. For us, the same could be true, and in many places is. Or the enemy could be *inside* the city gates—forces at work among us and between us, seen and unseen. The addiction to wealth and power at all costs, for example. Or white supremacy and other systemic injustices. Or the myth of scarcity that creates economic disparities between rich and poor. Or the greed that fuels our climate crisis and environmental destruction.

These are the enemies alive and unleashed in our world. They are fierce invaders, and they mean to capture and kill whatever pieces of us they can claim. A rampart-shaped pulpit reminds us of what's at stake: bodies, minds, souls, and spirits. When we are the ones called to the ramparts to speak, our job is to stand watch and wake the people from sleep, alerting them to the dangers massing at the city gates. We may have to wake God, too, if God seems to be absent or silent. We may have to break *God's* silence with loud cries to the heavens that summon God into action (see "L is for Lament").

In peacetime, preaching has the luxury of taking many forms. It can be a slowly unfolding conversation that builds quietly, incrementally, over the years. It can be a patiently constructed argument that takes months to unfurl. It can be unhurried attention to details, recorded with painstaking accuracy. It can be a wondrously open dialogue that has all the time in the world.

But in wartime, preaching necessarily takes on a kind of urgency and speed. The quality of time is different; things are heated and compressed. The rampart-shaped pulpit is up on the battlements. The preacher's words have longer and farther to travel to be seen and heard, and people are moving quickly; cannons are booming. There's no time for the fancy or overwrought.

Write the vision. Make it plain upon tablets, so a runner can read it.

In the end, Habakkuk's question ("Where will you stand?") isn't just for preachers. It's for all of us. When the times are dire and the backdrop is war, any one of us might be called to a rampart and given a vision. And tablets, to make it plain.

I

IS FOR

ISRAEL

Genesis 32

Jacob was left alone, and a man wrestled with him until day-break. When the man saw that he did not prevail against Jacob, he struck him on the hip socket, and Jacob's hip was put out of joint as he wrestled with him. Then he said, "Let me go, for the day is breaking." But Jacob said, "I will not let you go, unless you bless me." So he said to him, "What is your name?" And he said, "Jacob." Then the man said, "You shall no longer be called Jacob, but Israel, for you have striven with God and with humans and have prevailed."

Gen. 32:24–28

*J*acob is arguably the central figure in the book of Genesis. He certainly gets the most airtime: born in chapter 25, he lives to a ripe old age, dies with his twelve sons at his side and is buried in chapter 50, at the very end of the book. In truth, it takes that long to record the story of his family. And despite all the chapters devoted to telling it (and the fact that it's nearly impossible to put down, once you start reading), we never do seem to get to the bottom of who Jacob is, what makes him tick, and why controversy seems to multiply in his household. Jacob is a puzzle, as entertaining as he is confounding. He can charm us in one scene, scandalize us in the next, and move us to tears in between. We never quite make up our minds about him: is he a hero? An antihero? And we never get answers to all our questions about why God chooses someone like Jacob in the first place. How does a scoundrel and a thief who cheats his own brother get a place among the patriarchs as an exemplar of faith? God has reasons, but they aren't always accessible from where we sit.

In chapter 32, we have a story that marks a turning point in Jacob's life and gives us a key into his inner life as well. The insight we're given is this: Jacob is a man who will stay up all night to wrestle with a stranger who might be God.

"Wrestle" is the key verb here. It's what Jacob does his whole life: wrestle for a place, a profit, an advantage, and a blessing. He doesn't always fight fair, as some of the earthier translations of his Hebrew names are frank to say. At birth, he is called Jaakov/Jacob: "Heel-Sneak." Years later, in midlife, God gives him the name Yisrael/Israel: "God-Fighter."[1] Whether God sees this as progress isn't entirely clear. Yet both names lift up that wrestling aspect of Jacob's nature and speak to a shift in how he embodies it—and there *is* a shift as he grows older. In chapter 32, Jacob the Heel-Sneak, a man who lives and wrestles like a sneaky heel, becomes Israel the God-Fighter, a man who lives and wrestles mostly with God. The names describe two distinct ways of being in the world and grappling with the world.

Jacob is literally born wrestling, and losing that first match is the defining moment of his life. Esau, his twin brother, beats him to the gate, despite a neat heel-grabbing move on Jacob's part in the final push. Jacob earns his name in that tussle to be firstborn (to his family, he's Heel-Sneak), but not the coveted title of oldest son, and the experience makes him a fighter. His primary objective from then on is to win God's blessing and come first doing it. Even if the contest is within his family (it is) and he has to be a Heel-Sneak wrestler to do it (he does). Even if the aftermath brings family division (it will) and painful years of separation (it does). Even if he learns, to his dismay, that there are other Heel-Sneak wrestlers in the family who don't play fair either (there are), and he will have to be a bigger Heel-Sneak, or perhaps a God-Fighter with deeper skill and purpose, to survive (he will).[2]

1. Everett Fox, *The Five Books of Moses: A New Translation with Introduction, Commentary, and Notes,* Schocken Bible 1 (New York: Schocken Books, 1995), 155.

2. See the stories of Jacob and Esau (Gen. 25:29–34); Jacob, Esau, Rebekah, and Isaac (27:1–45); and Jacob and Laban (29:15–30; 30:25–43; and 31:1–16).

When our story in chapter 32 begins, Jacob is at a real low point. It's the night before his reunion with Esau, who decades ago suffered firsthand the damage his Heel-Sneak brother could do. Jacob is anticipating the consequences. He can't imagine that forgiveness could be on the table all these years later. He can't imagine that love might still be present. He is truly terrified, maybe for the first time in his life, that his wrestling ways have failed him and something new is required. He doesn't have language for it, except that what he wants is a blessing, and the One he needs to wrestle, now, is God. There isn't any way forward except to begin. To wrestle as he never has, for something he never knew he could want.

Jacob goes into that night feeling the most alone he has ever felt. He walks out of it limping, yet strong in spirit. God, it turns out, is a worthy opponent (if it *was* God; he can't be sure) and not above getting in a few licks (if Jacob's sore hip is any indication). God has also given him a name, a blessing, and plenty to think about. Maybe beating his opponent in a marathon match wasn't the goal. Maybe being a *partner* in that marathon match is the alternative he's been shown—that striving with God and human beings can look like more than dominating and accumulating. It could simply be . . . embracing. Receiving and offering blessing. Striving to be, and remain, in relationship, which might be the only thing worth fighting for, on earth or in heaven.

In some ways, Jacob is changed by this experience. In others, he's as stubbornly intractable as ever, "human," as biblical scholars often leave it, when fallible Jacob tests their patience. And it's hard to watch the Heel-Sneak part of his character seeping down into his twelve sons and the God-Fighter part so conspicuously lacking, while Jacob does nothing about it. He seems unable to transmit to his boys the lessons he's learned, with tragic consequences. It costs the family years of suffering and heartbreak (see "J is for Joseph" and "T is for Tamar").

But we do know this: "Israel" is the name passed down to Jacob's descendants and the nation that will arise. God-Fighter is the identity passed down to us. And maybe that part of us is worth striving for—to be a person who will stay up all night to embrace a stranger who might be God.

J

IS FOR

JOSEPH

Genesis 50

Realizing that their father was dead, Joseph's brothers said, "What if Joseph still bears a grudge against us and pays us back in full for all the wrong that we did to him?" So they approached Joseph, saying, "Your father gave this instruction before he died, 'Say to Joseph: I beg you, forgive the crime of your brothers and the wrong they did in harming you.' Now therefore please forgive the crime of the servants of the God of your father." Joseph wept when they spoke to him. Then his brothers also wept, fell down before him, and said, "We are here as your slaves." But Joseph said to them, "Do not be afraid! Am I in the place of God? Even though you intended to do harm to me, God intended it for good, in order to preserve a numerous people, as he is doing today. So have no fear; I myself will provide for you and your little ones." In this way he reassured them, speaking kindly to them.

Gen. 50:15–21

*J*oseph is the only biblical patriarch to have his own hit musical and DreamWorks video. That makes him better known to Broadway and young audiences than he might be in your average church—or a version of him, anyway. The amazing Technicolor King of Dreams Joseph we meet on stage and screen is winsome and earnest, a boy we can't help cheering for as he plows his way through classic Aristotelian plot structure (exposition, complication, resolution; or boy has all, boy loses all, boy wins it all back, plus millions in Egyptian gold) to a catchy musical score. It's vacation Bible school material, singable family fun. Nothing wrong with that.

But it does leave Joseph in a bit of a bind—another pit, to extend the biblical imagery. He never gets out of costume and makeup, and he's never free of the relentless Hollywood pressure to live happily ever after, no matter what. Life doesn't work that way. Neither does Scripture. Joseph's story is intended to speak to people who are at the bottom of a pit themselves, pummeled and broken and losing hope. It contains a "theology of beginnings," as biblical scholar Kathleen O'Connor so beautifully writes, "to convince its audience that the Creator of the cosmos and of all that exists is recreating them now."[1] Happy endings have nothing to do with it, and Joseph, a man who was pushed down and required to begin again multiple times, would be the first to confirm that. In the fiftieth chapter of Genesis, he does, in the famous words he speaks to his brothers about why he believes his life has turned out the way it has. He doesn't come to any easy conclusions, and it wouldn't be Scripture if he did. But he shows us how the grown-up, offstage version of Joseph is trying to make meaning of a life fractured and re-created.

Joseph's words in that chapter show us something else too: it matters, it matters a *lot,* who translates them. Reading a different biblical translation of Genesis 50:19–20 can be like watching a completely new production of Joseph when you know the old one by heart. It's a whole new play, with new upsets and insights. And when we're talking about the theological climax of a story, as these verses are, even the subtlest changes can cause dramatic shifts in meaning.

Joseph and his brothers are in Pharaoh's court at the time our scene in chapter 50 takes place, and Joseph is one of Pharaoh's high officials. How he got there is a long story, but it involves just about every horror one can imagine (massive family dysfunction, violence, betrayal, enslavement, false arrest, prison, global famine, and a dazzling rags-to-riches turnaround). Joseph has forgiven his brothers for the evil they did years before in selling him into slavery, and they in turn have worked through their childhood resentments about Joseph being their father's spoiled and best-dressed favorite. The plan, given the climate emergency, is for them all to live together in Egypt, the

---

1. Kathleen O'Connor, *Genesis 1–25A*, Smyth & Helwys Bible Commentary 1 (Macon, GA: Smyth & Helwys, 2018), 2–3.

only place left to buy grain, thanks to Joseph and his mysterious gift for interpreting dreams. But the brothers are worried. What if Joseph changes his mind about forgiving them? What if the tragedies in his life haunt him or drive him to seek retributive justice? They wouldn't blame him if he did. How, they wonder, can Joseph live with the appalling things he has had to endure at his brothers' hands? By which they mean—and they hardly dare whisper it—how can he live with *them*?

Joseph responds with gentleness, as we see in three renderings of his words in Genesis 50:19–20. Notice how they are similar at first but then diverge in significant ways. The middle line is the linchpin (italics mine).

Fear not, for am I instead of God? *While you meant evil toward me, God meant it for good,* so as to bring about at this very time keeping many people alive.

Robert Alter[2]

Do not be afraid! For am I in place of God?
Now you, you planned ill against me,
(but) God planned-it-over for good,
in order to do (as is) this very day—
to keep many people alive.

Everett Fox[3]

Don't be afraid. Do I act for God? *Don't you see, you planned evil against me but God used those same plans for my good,* as you see all around you right now—life for many people.

Eugene Peterson[4]

Joseph isn't offering his brothers cheap grace and a theological shortcut. He isn't minimizing the evil they have done or ducking the hard work of repair that goes hand in hand with forgiveness. He

2. Robert Alter, *The Five Books of Moses: A Translation with Commentary* (New York: W. W. Norton, 2004), 295.

3. Everett Fox, *The Five Books of Moses: A New Translation with Introductions, Commentary and Notes,* Schocken Bible 1 (New York: Schocken Books, 1995), 237.

4. Eugene Peterson, *The Message: The Bible in Contemporary Language* (Colorado Springs, CO: NavPress, 2005), 80.

isn't saying the whole thing was God's will, either, or "Everything turns out for the best!" Yet it's remarkable how often his words are misquoted, contorted, and then emblazoned on inspirational pillows and greeting cards, with a soppiness that would make the grown-up offstage Joseph gag. It's simple to do, if you truncate that italicized middle line, *While you meant evil toward me, God meant it for good,* and cut the first half so that it reads *God meant it for good*—which veers dangerously close to "God meant it," or "God meant for this awful thing to happen to *you,*" or even "This was God's will, so quit asking questions!" Misquote Joseph in that way, and we're back to those pillows and greeting cards.

Misappropriate the words, and we have another, more sinister problem: justifying oppression and enslavement in the name of God. That's simple to do too, if you take Joseph's truncated line and give it to his brothers to speak. *God meant it for good* on the lips of the oppressor sounds like a menacing preamble to more oppression and abuse; very often, it is. Steal Joseph's words in that way, and we are nowhere near a theology of beginnings.

Here is where translation makes a difference. Take a look at the second two renderings of Genesis 50:19–20: the word "meant" changes to "planned." One small revision, one choice to translate a word differently (in this case, the Hebrew *hashabah*), and we have an entirely new way to hear the text: *You planned one thing, but God planned it over,* to focus on Everett Fox's wording.

Meaning a thing and planning a thing are two different acts. Planning a thing is also different from "planning it over" (that is, going back to the drawing board to come up with plan B, which usually indicates that plan A was a flop). This Fox translation offers us another way to understand God's intentions and actions in relation to human intentions and actions. It also keeps us from easy assertions that what we intend, God intends; that our plan, whatever it is, had God's blessing and input from the start; that God meant for it to happen all along, because it was all part of God's megaplan for us. Yet the exact opposite may be true. Sometimes God steps in to rework the mess we make, in ways we can't immediately see. God plans it over, for another purpose. *Now you, you planned ill against me, but God planned-it-over for good.*

One reason this matters so much for us today is that Joseph and his brothers are reckoning with a major rift in their family that happened years ago, involving some of the worst harm a human being can do to another: selling a brother into slavery. We know something about that. We know what it is for nations and institutions to reckon with the evil of human enslavement and how structurally embedded it has been. We know that evil was planned. We know it was planned against some to benefit others, and then enacted for generations with vicious cruelty. We know it was even held up as God's plan for all of us: "God meant this for good," some said. Those words, Joseph's words, were stolen and twisted by Joseph's brothers and preached without repentance or shame. We know that in some places they still are. And the question now that we don't know how to fully answer is what to do, how to live, in the shadow of these appalling things. When Joseph's brothers intended such harm and planned such ill, what can be planned-over for good?

We don't have any easy conclusions, and it wouldn't be Scripture, or life, if we did. But Joseph's story may give us some clues. What does it mean to live into a theology of beginnings? What does it require to do the hard work, separately and together, of telling and listening to stories of inherited pain? How will we dream the dreams that lead to planning-over for good? Can we speak words that don't sound like they were lifted straight from the greeting card aisle?

We might have the barest chance—if we are brutally honest with ourselves, and can steer clear of a few things. Cheap grace, thrills, and shortcuts, for example. Stolen and twisted words. The amazing Technicolor song-and-dance ending to a show with a running time of two hours and fifteen minutes, including intermission. A hit musical is fun, but it isn't planning-over for good. We'll need more time and choreography than that to do the work of dismantling and then creating our next communal script.

K

IS FOR

KING SOLOMON

1 Kings 4

> God gave Solomon very great wisdom, discernment, and breadth of understanding as vast as the sand on the seashore. ... He composed three thousand proverbs, and his songs numbered a thousand and five. He would speak of trees, from the cedar that is in the Lebanon to the hyssop that grows in the wall; he would speak of animals, and birds, and reptiles, and fish.
>
> 1 Kgs. 4:29–33

*K*ing Solomon asked for wisdom, and this surprised the Lord. Apparently, young monarchs are more inclined to ask for things they can use in the next five minutes, rather than things that develop slowly over time. Money, power, and sleek new yachts tend to win out over wisdom, discernment, and breadth of understanding. Yet Solomon chose the latter, which surprised and pleased the Lord. Even as a young man, Solomon defied his demographic. He understood that the best quality for a leader is to see the world deeply and truly, in all its manifold patterns: to take the long and intricate view, as God might.

Solomon's wisdom was legendary. People came from far and wide to listen to him talk, and as Scripture says, he could talk about practically anything. He had knowledge of the vast natural world, which, as the Celts would later put it, was God's big book. Solomon knew Scripture, too—God's little book, according to the Celts—and added to its volume with songs and proverbs. He was a poet and a sage, a musician and a lyricist, a writer and a scholar of the world around him. He was, one might say, a homiletical naturalist.

Solomon proclaimed the wisdom of the earth. On his lips, it was the same as the wisdom of God, and why shouldn't it be? God created the strength and majesty of fragrant cedar wood, timber for a holy temple. God created the hardy abundance of medicinal hyssop, balm for a wounded messiah. Each was a gift to human beings, and each had something to teach about power. Cedar displayed it in height and breadth and beauty of grain; hyssop, in practical resilience, the fact that it could grow anywhere. God had ordered the world thus, with big and small purposes waiting to be uncovered. Those purposes were dependent on one another. They complemented one another. The temple might be built of cedar, but with a branch of hyssop, it could be purified. Everything in the natural world had a place, which inspired awe and wonder and praise: the speech of the wise.

You might think that standing in the tradition of King Solomon means aspiring to grand and glorious things. After all, Solomon possessed all the markings of success: immense wealth, grand building projects, fabled statesmanship, an international reputation. Everything he did, from marrying seven hundred princesses to hosting the queen of Sheba, was an act of shrewd diplomacy, calculated to ensure Israel a peace and prosperity it had never known (see "Q is for the Queen of Sheba"). You might assume that standing in his shoes as (for example) a preacher would be to head to the nearest tall-steeple church, sign up as their pulpit prince, and start a capital campaign.

But this isn't the case. Scripture gives more weight to what Solomon asked for as a young man than to what he possessed as an old one, and what he *first* asked for, what he wanted most, was wisdom. He wanted the long view: to see the earth slowly, rather than consume it quickly. To make deep connections where others might find none. To speak of God's creation as a man in love with every piece of it. Standing in the tradition of King Solomon means spending our lives in a state of wonder, not accumulation.[1] So what might that look like?

We might begin by spending more time in the books of the Bible that bear Solomon's name and association. The literature of wisdom—Proverbs, Ecclesiastes, the Song of Songs, the book of

1. William P. Brown writes that *wonder* is the beginning of wisdom. See *Wisdom's Wonder: Character, Creation, and Crisis in the Bible's Wisdom Literature* (Grand Rapids: Eerdmans, 2014).

Job—isn't read much in many faith communities. It comes up in the lectionary only infrequently, as if the church were embarrassed by what we might read there. Yet this is the literature that asks big questions about life, love, and the meaning of existence: What is the purpose of life? What is our human place on God's earth? Why do bad things happen to good people? How do we make wise choices and avoid foolish ones, and what does the good life look like? Wisdom literature, the body of work associated with Solomon and his yearning to be wise, is an excellent place for us to dwell. A person can't enter its pages without pausing over its questions, wondering if the ones *we 've* been asking are big enough.

Big questions are only part of the picture, however. Wisdom literature is also interested in small things: the close-at-hand, homey, earthy observations that can only be attained by paying very close attention to the world around us. Standing in the tradition of King Solomon means being as interested in the details as we are in the broad view, and God, as the poets like to say, is in the details. God is in the lingering description of a beloved's body: her hair, like a flock of goats moving down the slopes of Gilead; his eyes, like doves beside springs of water, bathed in milk (Song 4:1; 5:12). God is in the careful documentation of the creatures of this earth: the bright feathers of birds, the sharp teeth of lions, the wild offspring of mountain goats, the flashing scales of Leviathan (Job 38–41). God is in the keen observations of community life: neighbors who gossip, workers who toil, children who play, spouses who love. God is even in the salty and wry sayings that make us laugh and then think long and hard—like these, from the book of Proverbs:

> Like a dog that returns to its vomit
> is a fool who reverts to his folly.
> 26:11

> As a door turns on its hinges,
> so does a lazy person in bed.
> 26:14

> Better is a dinner of vegetables where love is
> than a fatted ox and hatred with it.
> 15:17

A word fitly spoken
is like apples of gold in a setting of silver.
25:11

The details are what make us sit up and listen, and then recognize ourselves. A person who is skilled with details can bring the world to our doorstep and place it carefully in our hands.

These two things—stepping back to see broadly, stepping forward to see closely—could occupy us for a lifetime, and there would be a cheerful rhythm to each day. But as King Solomon's story illustrates, even this rhythm has its limits. There's a need, at a certain point, to say with more precision who *God* is, and who God is not, so that the details of the natural and human world aren't equated with or indistinguishable from those of the divine. King Solomon, in the end, took such a broad view of the holiness of things that he began to sacrifice at many altars. He saw the sacred in so many of them (including those of the gods of his many wives) that he lost all perspective. He let go the particularity of his own sacred story. He overlooked the commandments. This, we are told, did not please the Lord. When Solomon died, adversaries lay in wait to overthrow the kingdom, and very soon it was torn apart.

Standing in the tradition of King Solomon means we have a balance to maintain. In our search for wisdom—to see it, to name it, to preach it—we're to speak of the natural world, yes. We're to speak of trees and cedars and hyssop and so forth, because the God of Israel is available to us in the biggest questions and smallest details that we can perceive. But God is also *not* fully available in those things, or at least, not fully grasped. There's an obscurity that cloaks even that rhythm of stepping back to see fully and stepping forward to see closely. In the end, God is simply beyond human wisdom.

Yet we thirst for it, and even dare to speak. And this, as Scripture says, pleases the Lord.

L

IS FOR

LAMENT

Lamentations 1

> Is it nothing to you, all you who pass by?
>> Look and see
> if there is any sorrow like my sorrow,
>> which was brought upon me,
> which the LORD inflicted
>> on the day of his fierce anger.
>
> From on high he sent fire;
>> it went deep into my bones;
> he spread a net for my feet;
>> he turned me back;
> he has left me stunned,
>> faint all day long.
>
> Lam. 1:12–13

"*L*ament" is not a word that sits easily in some cultural contexts. It can be an act we avoid, suppress, or soothe into silence, rather than a practice we teach. If that last part sounds bewildering (a practice we teach?!—who wants to do it, let alone learn it?!), so would our bewilderment itself to our ancestors in the faith. For them, lamenting was as natural as breathing, sleeping, laughing, and weeping, and just as essential, in its season. There was "a time to be born and a time to die," as Ecclesiastes 3 puts it, "a time to mourn and a time to dance," "a time to keep silent and a time to speak." There was a time to lament, as well, and a way to do it: fully, honestly, openly, and faithfully. The book of Lamentations was one expression of that, and still is. And it remains one of the least-tapped, little-known resources we have for a life of faith—which will always include a time to lose and then to

49

mourn, simply because it is life. Human beings need to lament. We need to do it alone and in community, privately and publicly, at home and in worship. If that sounds strange to us, maybe it's a signal: there is a time for the book of Lamentations, and if we don't know where that book is or how to find it, this might be the time to look.

Grief is often an occasion when language disappears. We are stripped of speech; we have no words for what we're experiencing. It's why communal expressions of grief—funerals, wakes, beloved hymns and spiritual songs, even cards and casseroles at the door—are so powerful in those moments.

After the events of 9/11 in 2001, seminaries offered continuing education classes on lament and grief, and a flood of ministers from all backgrounds and racial ethnic identities showed up. They had come to an abrupt theological dead end, with nothing more to say; whatever they'd relied on in tragedies past sounded hollow and wrong, like a gospel of platitudes. Immersing themselves in the sacred literature of lament—sections of Job, Jeremiah, Psalms, and the book of Lamentations, in particular—was like receiving water in the desert, water from stone, for these ministers. They marveled at how the ancient writings voiced what they could not: words of absolute grief, with no restraint. Lament literature helped them to reclaim a gospel of hope.

Twenty years later, in the shadow of multiple crises—the climate emergency, the COVID-19 pandemic, white nationalism, gun violence, racism, xenophobia, and anti-Semitism—the same rediscovery is happening. It's happening in the streets, too, in protest movements that begin as public expressions of grief and rage. As theologian Cheryl A. Kirk-Duggan has written, lament creates an eschatological space that points us forward; we can declare, together, that this is *not* the end of the story.[1]

In its day, the book of Lamentations was what we might call poetry of witness:[2] testimony, in poetic form, to the terrible suffer-

---

1. Cheryl A. Kirk-Duggan, "Lament as Womanist Healing in Times of Global Violence," in *The Oxford Handbook of Feminist Approaches to the Hebrew Bible*, ed. Susanne Scholz (New York: Oxford University Press, 2021), 154.

2. Poet Carolyn Forché introduced this term in 1993 in the introduction to an anthology that she edited, *Against Forgetting: Twentieth-Century Poetry of Witness* (New York: W. W. Norton, 1993), 29–47.

ing endured by the people of Judah during the Babylonian siege and destruction of Jerusalem. The five chapters of the book are really five poems, each one its own howl of pain, and each unbearably beautiful, in language and honesty. The narrator doesn't hold back anything or spare us anything. We get the whole searing account and the full force of emotion, in brutal detail. So does God. And surrounding all of this, holding each poem lightly yet firmly, is a carefully constructed form that functions like skin, like bone; it allows the words to pour out without bleeding out. Four of the poems are acrostics, each stanza starting with a letter in the Hebrew alphabet: it's lament, A to Z. The last poem breaks this pattern and even ends midsentence, as if to say, *no form, no words, can express the depth of this grief.* The form itself teaches. Lament needs some kind of structure—a rhythm we can enter into, a holding vessel like the community itself—to gently guide us toward speech and God, when the wilderness of grief has taken both.

The five poems in the book of Lamentations show us something else: suffering persons need room to speak *to* God and *about* God, not to blame—lament isn't blaming God for events that cause suffering—but to give voice to pain, grief, and anger. In these poems, the narrator addresses God directly and candidly. Most of that speech is what Walter Brueggemann calls "counter-testimony": telling the truth about how God seems to be absent and silent, and crying out to God (and even yelling at God) to cut it out and get back in character.[3] Counter-testimony is the equivalent of "How long, O Lord?" and "My God, my God, why have you forsaken me?" It goes hand in hand with what Brueggemann calls "core testimony": telling the truth about how God is always present, always moving in the world with justice and compassion. Core testimony is our central affirmation of faith, the equivalent of "God is great, and God is good!" God creates and calls, saves and delivers, hears and gives, loves and raises up. Core testimony and counter-testimony witness to Israel's honest *experience* of God as well as Israel's *hope* in God, both of which are necessary and need to be held together. Otherwise, God

3. "Core testimony" and "counter-testimony" are Brueggemann's terms for describing the nature of utterance—the way Israel speaks of and to God—in the Hebrew Bible. He finds that the same pattern holds true in the New Testament. See *Theology of the Old Testament: Testimony, Dispute, Advocacy* (Minneapolis: Fortress, 1997).

becomes an idol, only one thing. We won't be telling the full story of our lives and the truth of faith—which is that we know, we trust, we hope in the greatness and goodness of God. But we also wait for it and lament its absence. There is a time for core testimony and a time for counter-testimony.

Most of what we read in the book of Lamentations is counter-testimony: poems that speak to the bitterness of suffering. But now and then, as is true in life, a memory of core testimony bubbles up to the surface, interrupting the lament with a fleeting glimpse of hope.

> The thought of my affliction and my homelessness
>   is wormwood and gall!
> My soul continually thinks of it
>   and is bowed down within me.
> But this I call to mind,
>   and therefore I have hope:
>
> The steadfast love of the LORD never ceases,
>   his mercies never come to an end;
> they are new every morning;
>   great is your faithfulness.
> "The LORD is my portion," says my soul,
>   "therefore I will hope in him."
>
> The LORD is good to those who wait for him,
>   to the soul that seeks him.
>
> Lam. 3:19–25

Should it startle us that one of the best-loved hymns in the Christian tradition, "Great Is Thy Faithfulness," comes straight from the book of Lamentations, that a tragedy of epic proportions inspired words of utter despair as well as unbelievable hope? Not at all. Lament gives voice, even as it helps us come to voice. It does the same with hope. And it may be the only way forward, the only way back, the only way through, when the time to mourn comes.

M

IS FOR

MEMORY

Deuteronomy 6

Hear, O Israel: The LORD is our God, the LORD alone. You shall love the LORD your God with all your heart and with all your soul and with all your might. Keep these words that I am commanding you today in your heart. Recite them to your children and talk about them when you are at home and when you are away, when you lie down and when you rise. Bind them as a sign on your hand, fix them as an emblem on your forehead, and write them on the doorposts of your house and on your gates.

Deut. 6:4–9

*C*ommitting Scripture to memory isn't something many of us do anymore. Our grandparents and great-grandparents may have had to, if they went to Sunday school; a few generations back, it was standard practice for children to memorize key passages and recite them on command. Some churches still conduct "sword drills" or other competitive games for learning the books of the Bible, but rote memory work doesn't get the emphasis it once did. Maybe we got tired of the hard work it requires. Maybe we started to argue about which verses were the most important for our children to learn. Or maybe we read Mark Twain, who wrote a hilarious scene in *The Adventures of Tom Sawyer* about how ridiculous memorizing can be. In Tom Sawyer's Sunday school class, children would recite Bible verses and exchange them for tickets (a common practice at the time); two thousand tickets would earn them a Bible, presented with much pomp and ceremony. Tom hated memorizing but loved pomp and ceremony, so he figured out a way around the system: he enticed other boys to trade him their tickets for a chance to whitewash his fence. One morning in Sunday school, Tom waltzed up to his teachers with two thousand tickets, and they had to fork over the Bible—even though they knew perfectly well, to their great chagrin, that he hadn't memorized a single verse.[1]

In ancient Israel, memorizing Scripture was a part of life, but about as far from Tom Sawyer's Sunday school class as one can possibly get. There was a distinction to be made, they knew then, between *memorizing* and *memory*. Memorizing allowed them to learn by heart—and so commit to memory, in both body and soul. It taught them to think critically, act ethically, and live fully. And so from childhood to old age, people memorized Scripture. They learned wise sayings and proverbs. They recited the psalms. They recounted the Exodus stories of the mighty acts of God. It was what Moses had told them to do: *Keep these words in your hearts. Recite them to your children. Talk about them, at home or away. Write them on your doorposts and your gates.*

The process of memorizing and committing to memory helped Israel affirm some things about the life of faith.[2] One was that reciting Scripture by heart wasn't the same as taking it to heart along with all the mystery and wisdom within its pages. It would be the height of foolishness to think there was something magical about memorizing, as if it could automatically make a person wise (as in, "Correct extraction of doctrine: *check*. Plateau of truth: *check*."). If that were true, we might as well set up ticket booths all over town. Wisdom will never be about word-perfect recitation: what *we* are saying. Wisdom is about deep discernment: what the words themselves are saying. And the point is to do that work of discernment. To wonder at the mysterious wisdom of God and the limits of human understanding. To keep an open mind and to listen with focused attention. To develop our powers of observation and sympathy and

---

1. See chap. 4, "Showing Off in Sunday School," in *The Adventures of Tom Sawyer* by Mark Twain, first published in 1876.
2. These insights into the role of memory in Israel's life of faith come from Hebrew Bible scholar John Eaton. The next three paragraphs draw on his work. See "Memory and Encounter: An Educational Ideal," in *On Prophets' Visions and the Wisdom of Sages: Essays in Honour of R. Norman Whybray on His Seventieth Birthday*, ed. Heather A. McKay and David J. A. Clines (Sheffield: Sheffield Academic Press, 1993).

critical reflection. These are the deep mysteries we seek, and so we take Moses' counsel. *Keep these words in your hearts. Talk about them, at home or away.*

Israel also knew that memorizing Scripture was part of a God-given obligation, so that God's people will remember their own story. We need to remember the events that brought us up out of Egypt, through the wilderness, and into a promised land. And this kind of remembering is never indoctrination or hero worship. We are called, every day, to *live* in our own story, to learn it, recite it, and hand it down. To sit around the fire and tell the stories we most treasure. To bask in the warmth of a sacred truth-telling. When we do, memory is somehow bonded with the present. What happened then happens now; we live a story in multiple worlds—but only if we share what we've learned and pass those stories down. *Keep these words in your hearts. Recite them to your children.*

And finally, Israel discovered that memorizing Scripture brings us into communion with God. The words on the page aren't dried-up chaff for us to take in and spit out for tickets. They are a flood of grace, and the longer we spend with them, the deeper they go. When we learn Scripture by heart, it sinks down into our souls. When we commit the words to memory, it's like living inside a poem. Exactly as Moses once said: *Keep these words in your hearts. Recite them to your children. Talk about them, at home or away. Write them on your doorposts and your gates.*

N

IS FOR

NAOMI

Ruth 1

But Naomi said to her two daughters-in-law, "Go back each of you to your mother's house. May the LORD deal kindly with you, as you have dealt with the dead and with me. The LORD grant that you may find security, each of you in the house of your husband." Then she kissed them, and they wept aloud. . . .

> . . . But Ruth said,
> "Do not press me to leave you,
>   to turn back from following you!
> Where you go, I will go;
>   where you lodge, I will lodge;
> your people shall be my people
>   and your God my God.
> Where you die, I will die,
>   and there will I be buried.
> May the LORD do thus to me,
>   and more as well,
> if even death parts me from you!"

When Naomi saw that she was determined to go with her, she said no more to her.

Ruth 1:8–9, 16–18

*T*he book of Ruth is one of those rare delights in Scripture: a great story that features strong women in the main roles, a woman's name in the title, and a reliable spot on the biblical bestseller list. Only one other book in the Bible can make that claim (it's the book of Esther). Naomi and Ruth are so appealing as characters and their story so engrossing that the book remains a perennial favorite with audiences of all ages. It has drama and romance, which are always popular, and brevity, to make it a great *short* story: just four chapters. It has cautionary messages about power and exploitation, to start hard and necessary conversations.[1] And it has pride of place in many worship books as a suggested reading for weddings—which is where you're most likely to hear it. Many couples choose the words of Ruth 1:16–17 for their big day ("Where you go, I will go; where you lodge, I will lodge. . . ."), blithely unaware that they are *not,* as is often assumed, the glorious words of an epic love story. Instead, they are the glorious words of a woman to her mother-in-law, which doesn't make them any less powerful but does shift things slightly. It also gives us a teachable moment with humor and a fine opportunity to talk about the importance of context. What if we skipped past the factors that make for surface popularity and listened more closely to the book of Ruth, in its context and ours? How do those glorious words sound when we hear them in new places? How could they make a difference in people's lives when we speak them in new ways?

Since the book of Ruth is a great *short* story, it takes only a few minutes to read it in full and be up to speed, but here's a recap on how it opens. Naomi and her husband, Elimelech, are Hebrews who live in Bethlehem with their two sons. When their land is wracked with famine, the family decides to move east to Moab, where there is food and life. They stay for many years as alien residents, raising their sons in this foreign culture. In due time, the sons marry Moabite women, and it looks like the family may stay for good. But then disaster strikes. Elimelech dies. The two sons die. Famine strikes Moab. And the widow Naomi, who is now bereft of her husband, her sons, and any source of income, decides there is nothing left for her but to go back to Bethlehem and allow her daughters-in-law to return to their own mothers' houses. Maybe she knew that the women's best option for survival was to be given in marriage to new husbands. Maybe she just didn't want to be saddled with foreign

---

1. Carolyn J. Sharp, "Is This Naomi? A Feminist Reading of the Ambiguity of Naomi in the Book of Ruth," in *Feminist Frameworks and the Bible: Power, Ambiguity, and Intersectionality,* ed. L. Juliana Claassens and Carolyn J. Sharp (London: Bloomsbury T&T Clark, 2017), 149–61.

daughters-in-law, which would present its own challenges back in Bethlehem; we don't know. But the women weep as they say good-bye, and it's clear the daughters-in-law love Naomi and are grieving this farewell. One of them, Orpah, then does as Naomi directs and goes back to her mother's house. The other doesn't. Ruth, Naomi's Moabite daughter-in-law, who has never lived anywhere but Moab and is now facing the insecurity of an uncertain future in another country where *she* will be the alien—Ruth refuses to leave Naomi and let her go to Bethlehem alone. She won't hear of it. In fact, she promises to do the opposite: to stay, always. The scene feels sacramental, as Ruth clings to Naomi and speaks the well-known words: "Do not press me to leave you or to turn back from following you! Where you go, I will go; where you lodge, I will lodge; your people shall be my people, and your God my God. . . ."

To finish the recap on fast-forward, Naomi relents, and the women go on together, crossing the border into Bethlehem. Eventually, they secure a future for themselves through a series of events that will include field labor, surprise relatives, shrewd planning, and a make-it-or-break-it after-hours disrobing scene on the threshing floor; no commandments are broken, but intentions (among other things) are laid bare. Naomi's kinsman, Boaz, takes Ruth as his wife, and Ruth bears a son named Obed. But it's the women of the neighborhood who give the boy his name, because for them, he's Naomi's son. Ruth and Naomi will be foremothers of kings, from Obed to Jesse to David and his line.[2] The women of the neighborhood know that when God raises up a widow on her last shred of hope, and does it through her foreign daughter-in-law, for goodness' sake, it's a reason to celebrate by reinterpreting a few rituals.

And maybe that's exactly what our wedding liturgies are trying to express. Maybe those famous lines Ruth speaks to Naomi aren't just words, but *vows,* the most holy words we can say to another human being. And maybe Ruth's vow is one we should be speaking to more people on more occasions—*many* more than a wedding or a sacred family moment with a mother- or daughter-in-law, although these are good places to start. Maybe Ruth 1:16–17 is a suggested reading

---

2. See Matt. 1:5, and Matthew's account of Jesus' genealogy.

in our worship books because it's bigger than one couple's big day, and when the service ends, we're meant to take those words out and make a new vow ourselves. Maybe the point of putting the words in our worship books in the first place . . . is simply to *give* us the words. The rest is up to us.

Ruth's vow, if we can think of it that way, is an extraordinary one. She isn't promising to be a model of flexibility, the most easygoing daughter-in-law ever ("If you go to Colorado, I'll go to Colorado; if you stay the night in Bay Shore, I'll stay the night in Bay Shore—no problem"). She isn't promising to be a model of self-sacrifice, either, by giving up everything—her past, her present, her future, even her identity—in order to serve her mother-in-law. No, Ruth is promising a way of being present, of reorienting herself in human relationship, so as to give and receive from the other. *Where you go, I will go, and where you lodge, I will lodge.*

We might rephrase it like this:

> Wherever you choose to go, wherever you *have* to go,
> wherever you are cast out or driven to go, I will go there, too.
> Where you lodge and lay your head in weariness, I will lodge;
> I will stay there, and wait for you to wake.
> Whatever journey you must take, whatever wilderness you must
>   cross,
> I will go beside you, all the way to the other side.
> I will be present with you wherever you may be,
> and I will seek to know you in that place.

And so the questions come back to us: How do those glorious words sound when we hear them in new places? How could they make a difference in people's lives when we speak them in new ways?

One striking model is in Gabarone City, Botswana, where women have used the book of Ruth to create a ritual called a Naomi Shower.[3] Biblical scholar Musa W. Dube writes that the Naomi Shower is

---

3. Musa W. Dube, "Postcolonial Botho/Ubuntu: Transformative Readings of Ruth in the Botswana Urban Space," in *Transgression and Transformation: Feminist, Postcolonial and Queer Biblical Interpretation as Creative Interventions*, ed. L. Juliana Claassens, Christl M. Maier, and Funlọla O. Ọlọjẹde (London: Bloomsbury T&T Clark, 2021), 161–82.

intended for parents of a son or daughter who is getting married, and its purpose is to strengthen relationships in the family—and by extension, the whole community. This is particularly needed in southern Africa, where colonial practices of land reorganization have separated families and funneled them into workforces far from home, straining relationships at every level and tearing at the community spirit that sustains life. The Naomi Shower has had a hand in repairing and rebuilding these relationships, and it does this by highlighting aspects of Naomi's relationship with Ruth. The bridegroom's mother is the main focus of the shower; she is encouraged to take the lead in forging a strong bond with her new daughter-in-law. Participants share stories and wisdom, read from the book of Ruth and interpret it, and surround the new couple and both sets of parents with tangible and symbolic gestures of support. It's a moving event to witness, Dube writes, with rippling effects that reach deep into the community's heart. *Where you go, I will go, and where you lodge, I will lodge.*

The book of Ruth is that rare delight: Scripture that invites us to create something with it, something sacramental and new. A reading at a wedding. A ritual of healing. A vow of presence, as we begin again.

O

OLIVE LEAF

Genesis 8

> Then [Noah] sent out the dove from him to see if the waters
> had subsided from the face of the ground, but the dove found
> no place to set its foot, and it returned to him to the ark, for
> the waters were still on the face of the whole earth. So he put
> out his hand and took it and brought it into the ark with him.
> He waited another seven days, and again he sent out the dove
> from the ark, and the dove came back to him in the evening,
> and there in its beak was a freshly plucked olive leaf; so Noah
> knew that the waters had subsided from the earth. Then he
> waited another seven days and sent out the dove, and it did not
> return to him any more.
>
> Gen. 8:8–12

*N*oah and his family had spent the better part of a year on that ark,
living in close proximity to one another and a zoo's worth of animals.
The first forty days, they'd had the pouring rain and rising waters to
contend with, but once the rain stopped, there was nothing to do but
float over a world of water. For months and months, they were adrift,
waiting. And while an ark is spacious enough (this one was apparently the length of one and a half football fields, as wide as a tennis
court is long, and at least three stories tall), it's still a confined space
with no exits—and as far as Noah knew, no exit strategy. They were
alone in the universe with no place to land, and no land upon which
to disembark.

For a man who had done everything, up to now, exactly as God
had prescribed—from the building specs to the corralling and loading

of all those animals and provisions—Noah must have wondered whether God intended for them to just keep floating indefinitely. The Lord hadn't offered a single word of direction since the "I will blot out every living thing from the face of the ground" pronouncement (Gen. 7:4). But then one day Noah felt the ark come to rest on what turned out to be the mountains of Ararat, and in a few more months, he could see the tips of more mountains poking up from the waters. He opened the hatch and sent out a raven, and then a dove, to see what might happen. The raven went off on its own. But the dove, after two attempts, returned to Noah with an olive leaf in its beak—a sign of life and new things growing. Noah knew the flood was over and the waters had receded. They couldn't leave the ark yet, but in time they would; soon, and very soon. And sure enough, in a little while when the earth was dry, God finally gave the order and the blessing to go forth, that all the ark's living creatures might abound and be fruitful and multiply.

Waiting on God—for presence, guidance, or just the strength to keep going—is an experience every person of faith has, especially when we carry responsibility for others. And it can feel like waiting for dry land to appear while stuck in an ark for months. With the people and creatures God has given you for company and upkeep. After a ton of work on your part to build this structure and get everyone organized and on board. On a promise made long ago that God has a future in mind for all of you. Despite all that rain, and afterward all that water. Despite months of aimless floating and complete radio silence from the Lord. Despite your endurance and forbearance about the soundtrack that is constantly playing behind you: bleating and braying and honking and clucking and hissing and roaring and God knows what else. All that noise and all that waiting, and not even the hint of dry land or a word from the Lord.

You send out a raven. You send out a dove. Twice. Hoping they might sweep over the waters and find something you've missed, something you've failed to see from your bedraggled quarters. And finally, the dove comes back—not with a branch (or a full helping of presence, strength, and guidance), but with a single olive leaf. Something small and green, a slender shoot of hope. Something that lets you know the waters are receding, dry land is coming, and God does not, in fact, plan for you to drift along forever.

It isn't much to go on, one olive leaf shorn from its branch, but for Noah, it was enough. Not the same kind of "enough" the children of Israel learned in the wilderness, when they gathered manna each morning, enough for the day and no more. Manna requires a discipline of trust that God will provide what we need. Practice restraint today and we'll have bread tomorrow, and never have to wait longer than twenty-four hours.

An olive leaf is different. It requires a discipline of patience: God will bring us to dry land. Exactly *when,* we can't say—best guess might be "less than forever, more than twenty-four hours"— but maybe a lot more than that. Draining waters and growing green things take their own time. And while we can't hurry them, we can watch their progress. The waters ebbing, from seas to pools to puddles. The leaf growing, from sprig to branch to tree.

One olive leaf. One small sign of life. An indeterminate length of time to wait and to wonder. The rest—faith, hope, and love—is ours to nurture.

P

IS FOR

PUAH

Exodus 1

The king of Egypt said to the Hebrew midwives, one of whom was named Shiphrah and the other Puah, "When you act as midwives to the Hebrew women and see them on the birthstool, if it is a son, kill him, but if it is a daughter, she shall live." But the midwives feared God; they did not do as the king of Egypt commanded them, but they let the boys live. So the king of Egypt summoned the midwives and said to them, "Why have you done this and allowed the boys to live?" The midwives said to Pharaoh, "Because the Hebrew women are not like the Egyptian women, for they are vigorous and give birth before the midwife comes to them." So God dealt well with the midwives, and the people multiplied and became very strong. And because the midwives feared God, he gave them families. Then Pharaoh commanded all his people, "Every son that is born to the Hebrews you shall throw into the Nile, but you shall let every daughter live."

Exod. 1:15–22

*P*uah and her colleague Shiphrah were midwives to the Hebrew women in Egypt. They were in the business of delivering life, and when labor began in earnest, when it was time for professional help—someone with steady hands and a strong stomach who had been down this road a few times and knew what to do—they were the women to call. Puah and Shiphrah knew how blood-and-guts hard it was to bring new life into this world. They were prepared to wait with you, over that slow horizon of labor, and to be a witness through a long night with a lot of unknowns. And women who do this kind of work, day in and day out, don't scare easily.

Pharaoh hadn't foreseen that. He assumed anyone to whom he gave a direct order would be so terrified of him that they'd snap to, immediately, no matter what the order was—but he underestimated midwives. Puah and Shiphrah were trained to deliver life, not death, and they weren't about to shift course. When Pharaoh told them to kill any Hebrew boy they delivered, they went right out and didn't do it. When he asked them why, they lied to his face. It's the Bible's first recorded instance of civil disobedience: *The midwives did not do as the king of Egypt commanded.* And if we wonder how they ever got the courage to defy the most powerful man in Egypt, Scripture is remarkably matter-of-fact about it. One verb was all they needed: the midwives feared God. Not Pharaoh, God. And fear of the Lord is the beginning of wisdom.

Here's an interesting metaphor for a person of faith: *a midwife who fears God.* A person who is prepared to walk with others who are laboring. A person with steady hands and a strong stomach. A person who can see past the frenzy of the moment to what is waiting beyond that long horizon of pain. A person who knows how blood-and-guts hard it is to bring new life into this world. A person who believes that what seems physically impossible—there is no way new life is going to come out of a space that small—is, in fact, possible, because she's seen it, he's seen it; this is not their first delivery. A person who believes that even we in this moment are capable of delivering new life too.

A midwife who fears God. You have to be willing to relinquish the spotlight if you want that role. You aren't the one who's delivering. You're just the one they called to be a witness and an encourager and a professional set of hands at the ready. You have to watch the one who is laboring, and wait with them, however long it takes—and they will not be at their best. Twelve hours in, they will no longer be delighted to be experiencing the miracle of birth. They will hate everyone in the room, including you, for making them do this. You'll probably have to weather a lot of snarling and, later, screaming, because it hurts, and you are going to have to watch them hurt. Not forever, but long enough to tire you out and bring you to the point of exhaustion. Being a witness to a new creation is long, hard work, and a lot to clean up afterward.

A midwife who fears God. You have to match the verb to the right object, if you want that role. To fear God, and not Pharaoh and his administration. To fear God, and not the dark night of the soul. To fear God, and not the anxiety of all you do not know in this world (in other words, everything). A midwife who fears God sets those fears aside and endeavors to see the big picture—which is that this empire will not have the last word. It will not define the new order. It will not poison us with old hate. The only power we answer to is the Creator of the Universe and the God of love. The midwives weren't scared of Pharaoh! They feared *God*! And because of that, God gave them families—which in its broadest sense is a wider circle of human love, connection, and belonging than a person could ever have on their own.

A midwife who fears God. What if that's what *we* are supposed to be for one another, in these days? What if it's what we're supposed to be for the church, the nations, the earth itself? What if everything that is waiting to be born in you and in me is totally dependent on our willingness to walk with one another, behind the scenes, as a witness and another set of hands?

And what if the whole point of this . . . is to draw the circle bigger? *Because the midwives feared God, God gave them families.* God gave them more people to love. God gave them more people to claim. God gave them more people who, at the end of the day, would take them in—and that they would have to take in, too, no matter where those people had been, or what they'd done, or how they voted. God gave Puah and Shiphrah the condition of unconditional belonging to families they might never have chosen for themselves.

If this is the case, if this is the script we get, as a midwife who fears God, which families might God have in mind for us? Is it the older couple, long-standing pillars of the church, who have made it crystal clear that they think discussions of politics do not belong in the church? Is it the woman in her seventies, and the college student in her twenties, and the married mother of four, each of whom has wept while sharing a memory triggered by the #MeToo movement, a memory they thought they'd buried? Is it the kids in the confirmation class who declare the church doesn't listen to them or care about them, because if it did, if *we* did, we'd be doing something about climate change and the ecological disaster that's coming?

Are *these* the families God has in mind to give us, for being a midwife who fears God? Are these the people with whom we could share the state of unconditional belonging?! Yes. All of them; all at once. And a whole lot more we haven't mentioned, who are difficult, and controlling, and racist, and sexist, and filthy rich, and dirt poor, and gaming obsessed, and opiate addicted, and sexually abused, and falsely accused, and transitioning, and kicked out of their homes, and about to be fired, and on the brink of divorce—all those families too. And every one of them laboring to become some new creation. Every one of them ensuring us a long night and a lot to clean up.

It's wearing, yes. But also clarifying; love always is. It helps us match the verb to the right object. To *fear God,* for instance, rather than the church's extinction—so we can birth what the church might birth. Hang in there, with all this labor. Keep the long view—that the journey is tempered by what is waiting over that long horizon of pain: new life in Christ.

If we're ready for this—to be a midwife who fears God—then here's the covenant, when we get the call. Here's the job: Relinquish the spotlight, because it's their delivery. Be a steady witness who won't wear her heart on her sleeve. And get the script down, with the verbs in the correct order: *The midwives feared God, and that's what gave them courage. They did not do as the king of Egypt commanded, but they let the boys live.* That's the script: We let new life be. We don't try to control or even create it. We just create the space for it to come from someone else. We stand guard and protect them. We help them take that new life to their own home and raise it themselves—with love, we hope. And we know that new life raised with love grows into hope for all God's children. Every time a midwife says no to Pharaoh, we all get another chance.

The exodus out of Egypt begins like this. And Puah and Shiphrah, those audacious midwives, are at the head of the procession.

Q

IS FOR

THE QUEEN OF SHEBA

1 Kings 10

When the queen of Sheba heard of the fame of Solomon (fame due to the name of the LORD), she came to test him with hard questions. She came to Jerusalem with a very great retinue, with camels bearing spices and very much gold and precious stones, and when she came to Solomon, she told him all that was on her mind. Solomon answered all her questions; there was nothing hidden from the king that he could not explain to her. When the queen of Sheba had observed all the wisdom of Solomon, the house that he had built, the food of his table, the seating of his officials, and the attendance of his servants, their clothing, his valets, and his burnt offerings that he offered at the house of the LORD, there was no more spirit in her.

So she said to the king, "The report was true that I heard in my own land of your accomplishments and of your wisdom, but I did not believe the reports until I came and my own eyes had seen it. Not even half had been told me; your wisdom and prosperity far surpass the report that I had heard. Happy are your wives! Happy are these your servants who continually attend you and hear your wisdom! Blessed be the LORD your God, who has delighted in you and set you on the throne of Israel! Because the LORD loved Israel forever, he has made you king to execute justice and righteousness." Then she gave the king one hundred twenty talents of gold, a great quantity of spices, and precious stones; never again did spices come in such quantity as that which the queen of Sheba gave to King Solomon.

1 Kgs. 10:1–10 NRSV

*T*he queen of Sheba is the ancient world's original Power Woman: strong, independent, intellectual, politically shrewd, internationally connected, and ruler of a nation so rich that she could afford to travel from her home in Sabaea (present-day southern Arabia, Yemen, or Ethiopia) to Jerusalem in fabulous style: camels, jewels, spices, the works. She appears in the Hebrew Bible and the Qur'an, the New Testament and the writings of Josephus, and a vast array of tales, legends, and traditions that have flourished for two millennia in three major religions.[1] She is said to have been a philosopher, dark-skinned and ravishing. She was purportedly a convert to Judaism and also an ancestress of Islam. She hails from the same Ethiopian dynasty as Haile Selassie, it is said. And like Power Women everywhere, she's seen her strengths eclipsed by story lines that are less threatening—like romance.

It started with one verse. (It always does.) Ancient interpreters pounced on 1 Kings 10:13, "Meanwhile, King Solomon gave to the queen of Sheba every desire that she expressed"—a verse they heard as suggestive—and ran with it, to predictable ends. What started out as a state visit to a neighboring monarch is now a blockbuster love affair on the big screen, starring the latest heartthrobs of your choice.[2] The son from that union is said to have taken the ark of the covenant to Ethiopia.[3] And since rumors of a secret lovechild usually win out in the popular press, the queen of Sheba's night of passion with the dashing King Solomon is a folktale that persists, despite what Scripture says on that subject, which is nothing, really.

What Scripture *does* say is that the meeting of these two monarchs might have been like the coming together of two great minds of the age, rather like the meeting between Albert Einstein and Marie

---

1. See Matt. 12:42 and Luke 11:31 for the New Testament references. Titus Flavius Josephus was a first-century Jewish historian and citizen of Rome. Two of his works, *The Jewish War* and *Antiquities of the Jews*, have been important historical sources for first-century Palestine and for first-century Christianity, second only to the Bible.

2. In 1959, those heartthrobs were Yul Brynner and Gina Lollobrigida, who starred in *Solomon and Sheba*. The steamy poster tells all.

3. One source for more information is "The Queen of Sheba in History and Legend," a lecture by Annette Yoshiko Reed, currently professor of New Testament and early Christianity at Harvard Divinity School, presented at the Penn Museum in Philadelphia on April 6, 2016, https://www.penn.museum/collections/videos/video/4.

Curie in 1911. Had these two been men, their summit might not have attracted so much attention from anxious interpreters. The story of the queen of Sheba has a great deal more to show us than what we often hear, and it's every bit as fascinating as the torrid accounts of her lures and wiles. She is more than King Solomon's soul mate (as romantic as that might be), and she's more than someone high-and-mighty who needs to be taken down a notch (as in, "Who do you think you are—the queen of Sheba?"), much more. She's a person to seek, a person to emulate, for the balanced way she approaches life and her relationships with her peers.

This is a woman who doesn't hold back. When she has questions, she asks them. When she is skeptical of reports, she goes straight to the source—and she goes in peace, with deliberate gestures of goodwill and openness. She speaks directly to the person involved. She takes the time she needs to ask hard questions and the time she needs to listen. She draws her own conclusions, and she doesn't keep them to herself: when she's wrong, she says so; when she's impressed, she offers praise. She isn't threatened by the intelligence or gifts of another. To the contrary, she rejoices in them. And when she departs, she leaves blessings in her wake.

The queen of Sheba might be a surprising antidote to our social media age, when direct communication and open dialogue are sorely lacking—and are the very skills we need to relearn and practice. The queen's story is quite amazing, when we sit down and think about it. So is the fact that it's survived. And no embellishments to it, no matter how far-flung or fanciful, can detract from the core narrative, which is this: *When the queen of Sheba heard of the fame of Solomon, she came to Jerusalem herself, to test him with hard questions.*

Being tested with hard questions isn't the most comfortable way to spend a day. Tests can be stressful, as any seven-year-old will tell you. If the questions aren't relevant, if the learning goals and rubrics aren't clear, the experience is infuriating, just a spouting of nonsensical verse. But the tests we remember from long-ago school days were often more about reciting facts than demonstrating wisdom—and this is the difference in the queen of Sheba's testing of King Solomon. The queen was a seeker of wisdom. Her hard questions had to do with the deep logic of the universe. And she was prepared to observe everything, from the depth of his knowing to the interactions of his household, because we can't know a person without knowing how they live with others. *She came to Solomon and told him all that was on her mind. She came to Jerusalem herself, to test him with hard questions* (see "K is for King Solomon").

This vision of a deep exchange of minds, without anxiety or vindictiveness, might be brand-new for us, a world we haven't explored. But wouldn't it be a relief to live there—in a world where hard questions are allowed and respected, relevant and meaningful? Wouldn't it be welcome to have the trust and skills to initiate conversation, rather than avoiding it? Wouldn't it be a breath of fresh air if we believed that *being asked hard questions* isn't an affront or the road to more conflict, but really a compliment—and a road to greater insight?

It's a far cry from sliding sideways and muttering opinions to friends we know will agree—which is the world that's structured for us much of the time. There might be other ways to do it. And what a lovely reversal that would be, if a wise and royal ancestress from the ancient realm of Sabaea could teach us a little postmodern sense.

R

IS FOR

RAHAB

Joshua 2

Then Joshua son of Nun sent two men secretly from Shittim as spies, saying, "Go, view the land, especially Jericho." So they went and entered the house of a prostitute whose name was Rahab and spent the night there. The king of Jericho was told, "Some Israelites have come here tonight to search out the land." Then the king of Jericho sent orders to Rahab, "Bring out the men who have come to you, who entered your house, for they have come to search out the whole land." But the woman took the two men and hid them. . . .

Before they went to sleep, she came up to them on the roof and said to the men, "I know that the LORD has given you the land and that dread of you has fallen on us and that all the inhabitants of the land melt in fear before you. For we have heard how the LORD dried up the water of the Red Sea before you when you came out of Egypt and what you did to the two kings of the Amorites who were beyond the Jordan, to Sihon and Og, whom you utterly destroyed. As soon as we heard it, our hearts melted, and there was no courage left in any of us because of you. The LORD your God is indeed God in heaven above and on earth below. Now then, since I have dealt kindly with you, swear to me by the LORD that you in turn will deal kindly with my family. Give me a sign of good faith that you will spare my father and mother, my brothers and sisters, and all who belong to them and deliver our lives from death." The men said to her, "Our life for yours! If you do not tell this business of ours, then we will deal kindly and faithfully with you when the LORD gives us the land."

> Then she let them down by a rope through the window, for
> her house was on the outer side of the city wall and she resided
> within the wall itself.
>
> Josh. 2:1–4a, 8–15

Rahab has the lead role in Israel's second undercover mission to the land of Canaan, forty years after Moses directed the first one (see "C is for Caleb"). As a Canaanite herself, she was supposed to be a target. But she turned out to be a better spy than the two Joshua sent, who appear to have blown their cover the second they walked into Jericho and made Rahab's establishment their first stop—and why they did that is anyone's guess. Maybe they surmised (correctly) that a prostitute who lives inside the walls of a city would naturally have her finger on the pulse of the inhabitants. Maybe they were confident (incorrectly) in their ability to blend, and dizzy at the thought of a few unsupervised hours.

Whatever the reason, Rahab was onto the spies in no time, which was lucky for them, because everyone else was too; they hadn't managed to fool a soul. The king's men came asking questions, and Rahab was ready with a convincing story. She covered for them and, when the coast was clear, made her deal with the now compromised and greatly in-her-debt spies. As the two made their sheepish escape out her window and into the hills, Rahab placed a red cord in her window, at their instruction. It was an obvious yet symbolic bit of spycraft: the red cord was the sign that Israelite soldiers were to pass over Rahab's house, just as the angel of death had once passed over theirs in Egypt. When the city of Jericho fell, just as Rahab had foreseen, she and her family were the only ones spared.[1] Scripture reports that she lived in Israel from that day forward.

Rahab's reputation as a woman of courage and faith has remained largely intact through the centuries, which is saying something, given her triple-threat marginalized status ("harlot" is the big hit, but "woman" and "Canaanite" pack a punch too). Her story has always held a certain mystique. If some early interpreters were squeamish

---

1. See Josh. 2:1–24 and 6:17–25.

about her profession and preferred to think of her as an innkeeper, others weren't embarrassed at all to call her a prophet, a heroine, and the most beautiful woman in the world. She was said to have married Joshua and been an ancestor of Jeremiah. She is one of the four surprising women Matthew names in Jesus' genealogy.[2] She is the only woman to have her own entry in the Epistle to the Hebrews' roll call of faith.[3] Rahab is, on the face of it, Israel's favorite and most infamous convert.[4]

But she is also more complex than this and, for contemporary interpreters, more difficult to pin down. Much of that has to do with the very disturbing book in which her story is located: Joshua, the account of Israel's military conquest of the land of Canaan, which has to be one of the most terrifying books in Scripture. For too many years and in too many places, the book of Joshua has been read as a biblical text that authorizes violence in the name of chosenness (that is, God's chosen people, whose manifest destiny is to conquer a land and slaughter its inhabitants). Any text like that is in need of massive disruption.[5] Yet Rahab hasn't always been permitted to disrupt the theological toxins in her own story. As the Canaanite who converted, she's been held up as proof that the violence was justified; as the Canaanite who conspired, she's been called a collaborator and a sellout. In other words, a pawn in someone *else's* story, anything but disruptive. Which is not at all the person we meet in the second chapter of Joshua, who never asks permission of anyone.

Rahab is like a certain kind of stock character in literature: not the lord or lady of the manor, but the servant downstairs whose cleverness and ingenuity will eventually save the day. On the surface, those

2. See Matt. 1:5. Rahab holds court with Tamar (Gen. 38), Ruth (Ruth 4), and Bathsheba (2 Sam. 11), and gives Jesus a harlot in his family tree.

3. See Heb. 11:31.

4. For more of Rahab's reception history, see Amy H. C. Robertson, "Rahab and Her Interpreters," in *Women's Bible Commentary,* 3rd ed., ed. Carol A. Newsom, Sharon H. Ringe, and Jacqueline E. Lapsley (Louisville, KY: Westminster John Knox Press, 2012), 109–12.

5. For a helpful framing of the interpretive issues at stake, see Walter Brueggemann, "The God of Joshua: An Ambivalent Field of Negotiation," in *Joshua and Judges,* ed. Athalya Brenner and Gale A. Yee, Texts @ Contexts Series (Minneapolis: Fortress Press, 2013), 13–25.

characters may seem secondary and unimportant, but we underestimate them to our peril—as the owner of the house always discovers. They are often more noble than the nobility they serve. They possess strengths that show the weakness of the privileged house owner. And they work the edges of the story, in the passageways meant for servants, when the grand staircases and fine rooms are revealed to be empty facades. They may be maids or chauffeurs or chimney sweeps or prostitutes; it doesn't matter. The important thing is they're survivors—and the ones with the keys to *our* survival, as well.

Rahab is a character like this: a prostitute on the edges who lives inside the city walls, and who does what so many other on-the-edge characters in Scripture do. She sees a truth when others don't. She seizes her chance when others waver. And she survives; her life is saved, even though (and this is always an irony in Scripture) it wasn't a life many in her city would have thought or bothered to save. But as long as she has a chance, as long as she sees the merest opening, Rahab will keep pressing after others have given up the fight. In Scripture, that kind of persistence is seen as faith.

And Rahab is more. For us, as we read her story today, she is the downstairs stock character for *our* manor house. Rahab is an unseen, listening presence inside the walls of the things we human beings construct in the name of God. Our buildings. Our theologies. Our political platforms. Anything that delineates an "us" and a "them," anything that claims to know who is chosen and who is not, anything that sanctions divine violence as a final solution, is a hollow wall where Rahab needs to be listening—and plotting. If necessary, she may even be plotting against us. And in the end, that may be the very thing that saves our lives. Some texts, even *our* texts, are in need of massive disruption.

Rahab is the one to do it. She's the only one in this story who seems to know the first thing about disruption: how to change sides, choose allies, plan escapes, and betray her city, when these are necessary—so she and her family can survive. She's not the owner of the house. But she knows all the hidden passageways, and she's classic double-agent material. That red cord in her window is for us.

S

IS FOR

SALT

Genesis 19

When morning dawned, the angels urged Lot, saying, "Get up, take your wife and your two daughters who are here, or else you will be consumed in the punishment of the city." But he lingered, so the men seized him and his wife and his two daughters by the hand, the LORD being merciful to him, and they brought him out and left him outside the city. When they had brought them outside, they said, "Flee for your life; do not look back or stop anywhere in the plain; flee to the hills, or else you will be consumed." . . .

Then the LORD rained on Sodom and Gomorrah sulfur and fire from the LORD out of heaven, and he overthrew those cities and all the plain and all the inhabitants of the cities and what grew on the ground. But Lot's wife, behind him, looked back, and she became a pillar of salt.

Gen. 19:15–17, 24–26

*L*ot's wife might be cheered to learn that she isn't just a pillar of salt, as far as her reading public is concerned. She hasn't been universally condemned for looking back when she was instructed not to, and she hasn't been left to face her detractors by herself. The woman has more poets in her corner than any other Wife-of-Somebody in Scripture, and they are not about to let centuries of quite-certain critics have the last word. The poets aren't buying it, that it's okay to condemn a person for looking back without at least *asking* if she might have had her reasons. They are going to rewrite, revamp, and repair whatever interpretive damage has been done until Lot's wife is more than just an object lesson in disobedience. And they are serious about it. These are serious people with serious credentials, who write the sort of poems that win Nobel Prizes, Pulitzer Prizes, and honorary doctorates from Oxford. They know that imagination and theology go hand in hand. For them, it makes perfect sense that the health of a civilization depends more on the questions it asks than the answers it demands.

Why did Lot's wife look back? What a simple question that is, and an innocent one, at heart. It's the kind of question a child might ask after hearing the story read aloud and realizing (as children often do) that it's left out a few things—and inquiring minds want to know. Scripture frequently leaves things out. The gaps can be puzzling and just as interesting as the story. They're worth asking about, and children will, but adults don't always take the time. "Why did Lot's wife become a pillar of salt?" is an easy content question adults like to ask. It comes straight from the story, and the story gives us the answer: "Because she looked back, and she wasn't supposed to." *But why did she look back?* That's an imagination question the story doesn't answer, so we need to think about it—yet adults don't. They tell her she did wrong, but they don't ask her *why.* Which is puzzling to a six-year-old, who has already learned that when children do what they're not supposed to do, adults *always* ask why. And children always have reasons, and adults take those into account—which is to everyone's benefit.

This is the objection the poets raise: when it comes to Lot's wife, we make many assumptions and ignore the questions that matter. The result has been swift judgment and centuries of negative speculation—but over what her critics see as her unfortunate character, rather than her unfortunate circumstances. Many of them are confident that Lot's wife wasn't a nice person to begin with. They have outlined reasons why this must be so: she was a native of Sodom, unwelcoming to angels, fond of gossip, and borrowed too much salt from the neighbors. Those are theories that have circulated in high places. And what infuriates the poets is the ease with which her critics presume her guilt with conjectured proof. Why not the other way around? they ask. Why not presume her innocence, or even her humanness? At the very least, can we go back to the story to see what we might have missed?

The challenge here is that it's a disturbing story and flat-out painful to read. Only the middle chunk is printed above, and reading the whole chapter is the only way to get the full weight of it. (That said, Gen. 19 includes graphic accounts of mob violence, attempted rape, and incest, so please read carefully and at your discretion.) Lot's wife and her family—two daughters and Lot—were residents of Sodom, one of the cities in the verdant plain of Jordan. Lot had selected that portion of the land when he and his uncle Abraham agreed to part company; Abraham settled in the land of Canaan (see "U is for Ur"), while Lot moved to one of the wealthy cities on the plain. And like many urban centers, Sodom and its sister city, Gomorrah, let greed and pride run rampant. Injustice takes root everywhere. God hears the outcry over the inhabitants' sin and wickedness (which, incidentally, is not described in terms of same-sex love or homosexual acts) and, thoroughly incensed, slates the cities for destruction. Abraham manages to barter for the lives of Lot, his family, and any other righteous persons to be found, but Lot's family is it. Two angels are dispatched to rescue them.

The story becomes deeply troubling at this point. Lot shows hospitality to the angels, takes them into his home, and tries to protect them when a mob of angry men comes to the door, ready to storm the house. The men are furious that Lot's guests have a message of judgment for their city, and demand that Lot give his guests over to them, to deal with as they see fit.[1] Lot's response is to offer the men his two unmarried daughters instead—in the name of hospitality and preserving the honor of his guests. It doesn't come to that in the end; the angels intervene. But the scene is brutal and ugly, and we never hear what Lot's wife and daughters thought or said about any of it. Scripture is completely silent on the matter. All we know is that the next day, the angels take the family in hand to lead them out of the city. The orders are to get up, get out, and keep running for their

1. Poet Pádraig Ó Tuama, the host of "Poetry Unbound" on the *On Being* podcast, reminds us that this scene in Gen. 19 is one we see over and over again: angry men whose response to a message they don't want to hear about the injustice they don't want to see is to brutalize the messenger for daring to confront them. See his reflection on Natalie Diaz's poem "Of Course She Looked Back," in "Poetry Unbound," October 12, 2020, https://onbeing.org/programs/natalie-diaz-of-course-she-looked-back/.

lives, without looking back at the disaster behind them: their home and their city, their friends and those they loved, engulfed in flames and burning to the ground. Lot's wife is the only one who pauses as they make their escape, turning for one last look behind her. She is consumed on the spot, frozen in place and in salt. The family has to leave her behind too.

Why did Lot's wife look back? We are back to the question and the poets' challenge to imagine possible responses—and really, it's not so difficult to do. Human beings look back at all kinds of things, all day long. Historians look back at events. Detectives look back at clues. Therapists look back at childhoods. Insurance claims adjusters look back at photos of the damaged vehicle and the mechanic's repair estimate, to decide if the dent you got in the grocery store parking lot is covered, and for how much. And even if we don't look back for a living, we all look back as part of daily living—for our keys or gear or where we left the mail, and hundreds of other things so mundane we hardly even notice.

And we do it for good reasons, as the poets want us to see. So we can lock the door and leave the house. Look out for cars and cross the street. Check for footprints on the clean floor. Give a hug and wave good-bye. There are always reasons, and they have purpose and impact—which Lot's wife knew just as well as we do. And if we can't think of any reasons why *she* might have looked back (or if the only one we can think of is that she must have been a Very Bad and Disobedient Person), the poets have suggestions for us, to spur our imaginations:

> I looked back setting my bundle down.
> I looked back not knowing where to set my foot.[2]

> She wondered had she unplugged
>   the coffee pot? The iron?[3]

2. Wislawa Szymborska, "Lot's Wife," In *Poems New and Collected: 1957–1997* (New York: Ecco, 1998), 149–50.

3. Natalie Diaz, "Of Course She Looked Back." *When My Brother Was an Aztec* (Port Townsend, WA, Copper Canyon Press, 2012), pp. 88–89.

her head turned back as if in longing to be the girl
she had been in the city she had known.[4]

God spoke to Lot, my father.
She was hard of hearing. He knew that.[5]

But a wild grief in his wife's bosom cried,
Look back, it is not too late for a last sight.[6]

On the breast of the hill, she chooses to be human,
and turns in farewell—[7]

Of Course She Looked Back. That's the title of Natalie Diaz's poem about Lot's wife. And in the end, perhaps this is a clue to what the poets are pointing toward—that (in my words)

This could have been any of us.
It might still be any of us.
And looking back at burning ruins,
at destruction and holocaust,
looking back at what we loved as it is utterly destroyed,
is never weakness, but resistance;
never sin, but benediction:
a way to bless, and then go,
so we can honor what we must leave behind.

4. Gary J. Whitehead, "Lot's Wife." *A Glossary of Chickens* (Princeton: Princeton University Press, 2013), pp. 7–8.

5. Muriel Rukeyser, "Ms. Lot." *The Collected Poems of Muriel Rukeyser*, edited by Janet E. Kaufman & Anne F. Herzog, with Jan Heller Levi (Pittsburgh: University of Pittsburgh Press, 2005), p. 540.

6. Anna Akhmatova, "Lot's Wife." *The Complete Poems of Anna Akhmatova*, second edition, translated by Judith Hemschemeyer, edited and introduced by Roberta Reeder (Brookline, MA, Zephyr Press (2000), p. 273.

7. Kristine Batey, "Lot's Wife." Jim O'Brien, "Verbal Snapshots from Nine Years at the Free Press," *New England Free Press* (https://www.nefp.online/blank-1), accessed March 29, 2023.

Why did Lot's wife look back? For the same reasons we do. And when we see that, we have empathy—which is to say, humanity. We can read this story and know a truth about ourselves: we look back so we can move forward and then, if we can, move on. To be the ones alive, to imagine a future at all, is sacred. To ask the questions that might lead us to such a place is a privilege.

T

IS FOR

TAMAR

Genesis 38

About three months later Judah was told, "Your daughter-in-law Tamar has prostituted herself; moreover, she is pregnant as a result of prostitution." And Judah said, "Bring her out, and let her be burned." As she was being brought out, she sent word to her father-in-law, "It was the owner of these who made me pregnant." And she said, "Take note, please, whose these are, the signet and the cord and the staff." Then Judah acknowledged them and said, "She is more in the right than I, since I did not give her to my son Shelah." And he did not lie with her again.

When the time of her delivery came, there were twins in her womb.

Gen. 38:24–27

*T*he story of Tamar takes a chapter and an evening to tell properly. It carries the subtitle "Judah and Tamar" in many Bibles, but a better one would be ". . . It's Complicated," and that's putting it mildly. This is because Tamar, through time, circumstance, and no fault of her own, has to work her way through four men in the same family before she is given her due as a woman of honor: the right to bear children in her husband's house. It earns her a place in the family as the mother of twin sons and a place in the genealogy of Jesus. Open the Gospel of Matthew, and Tamar is the first woman mentioned in that list of forebears, making her the first woman to be named in the New Testament ("Abraham was the father of Isaac, and Isaac the father of Jacob, and Jacob the father of Judah and his brothers, and Judah the father of Perez and Zerah by Tamar"). It's almost as if Matthew expects that we'll know who she is—that her name is so important and her story so widely told, he can take it for granted we've already heard it and will understand, immediately, why Jesus' story must include hers.

There are several reasons why it takes an evening to tell Tamar's story properly. One is that young children are presumably in bed and asleep. Another is that we could be shocked or put off by some of the mature-audience details, and might even stop listening; we may need time to get a grip and some perspective. Still another is that we might start jumping to conclusions before the story is finished, especially if we get hooked and distracted by morality issues. That would be a mistake. Tamar is a prime example of why we say things like "Never judge a book by its cover" or "Those who live in glass houses shouldn't throw stones." The old proverbs hold true, in her case. So do new ones you can find on T-shirts, like "Don't judge my story by the chapter you walked in on," which she could have said herself, and essentially did. The bottom line is that to get to the crux of what Tamar has to show us, we have to wade through some seedy stuff, and it takes time. Most of it isn't about her at all. It's about the sorry men in her life who cannot and will not do the right thing.

Tamar isn't the first woman to be tied down to weak men, and she won't be the last. Two of them are so weak, in fact, that God slays them in disgust: Er, Tamar's husband, who apparently was "wicked in the sight of the LORD" (which is the only thing we know about him), and Onan, Er's younger brother, who apparently didn't take seriously his duty to his dead brother to get the widow pregnant in that dead brother's name (which is the reason God smites him: he helps himself to the widow, but pulls out, as it were, on the other duties). At this point, Tamar is still childless and running out of options. Her father-in-law, Judah, has promised to give her to Shelah, his youngest son, when Shelah is old enough—as tradition and obligation dictate for a widowed daughter-in-law. But Judah reneges on his promise, apparently out of fear that God will slay Shelah and he'll lose that boy too. Every man in this family has reneged and withheld for his own gain and profit, without a thought for the woman they have left behind. It's a pattern of behavior we've witnessed before. Tamar has been cheated out of her rights, as surely as others in this family were cheated out of theirs (see "I is for Israel"), and for Tamar, those rights were her only hope of financial security. Now she's on her own. Yet she doesn't seek revenge; she changes the state of play.

The plan she hatches is as brilliant as it is lurid, and it requires absolute composure. (Read the chapter for complete details. Gumption and mettle don't begin to cover it.) And the plan achieves its purpose; Tamar learns she is pregnant. Three months later, so does the rest of the family, and since they've walked in late and don't have the T-shirt, they don't hesitate to judge. But Tamar is incredible. She doesn't lie. She doesn't lash out. She simply unmasks, with a handful of objects that speak for themselves: Judah's signet, cord, and staff. "Take note, please, whose these are" is all she has to say.

Tamar lets Judah put the pieces together. She even has the grace to say nothing further, sparing him a public airing of the humiliating tale. And Judah, a man who pimped his own brother and sold him down the river, because he was jealous that his father never gave him a look; Judah, who was angry that his father reneged on *his* family obligations, out of love for one son to the neglect of the rest (see "J is for Joseph")—Judah finally gets it. He sees the truth that he is naked before the Lord. He sees the shame, his alone to bear, that he has not led his sons in the paths of righteousness. His daughter-in-law has had to defile herself to bring about justice for herself and her no-good dead husband (he has to admit that last part). Gumption and mettle indeed.

Judah acknowledges Tamar's courage publicly. "She is more in the right than I," he says, "since I did not give her to my son Shelah." Notice the wording: not "She is right," but "She is *more* in the right." In this family, that's a start. Justice comes about in more ways than we can dream or imagine. Even in ways it disgusts us to imagine.

So we have a little resurrection at the end of this story. Tamar raises up sons in the name of her no-good dead husband, yet the twins, Zerah and Perez, are Judah's boys. Their birth, just like that of their grandfather Jacob and *his* twin brother, Esau, features a last-minute wrestling match to be firstborn; history repeats.[1] But not all history. In Judah and Tamar's family, the cycle of pain is broken. There will be no more withholding of sons or blessings, and there

1. Compare Gen. 25:21–26 and 38:28–30.

will be no more judging if we haven't heard the whole story. Tamar's son Perez, by her father-in-law Judah, is recorded in the genealogy that leads straight to Jesus—to the *gospel* of Jesus—and are we really surprised? Jesus spent a lot of time with women like Tamar, who had complicated stories. He listened without judging. And he knew, from his own family and his family tree, that a story can take an evening to tell and hear properly. An evening, and a meal, with room for everyone around the table.

U

IS FOR

UR

Genesis 15

> Then he said to [Abram], "I am the LORD who brought you
> from Ur of the Chaldeans, to give you this land to possess."
>
> Gen. 15:7

*T*he ancient city of Ur was where Abraham was born, and where he and his wife, Sarah, lived until Abraham's father declared he was moving the family to the land of Canaan. To be clear, this wasn't a hop to the next county; Canaan was more than eight hundred miles from Ur, over mountains and rivers and deserts and a time zone. The little band set out and got as far north as Haran before deciding to stop and settle down for a few decades. Abraham and Sarah didn't resume the journey to Canaan until many years later, when they were in their seventies. That's like moving from New York to New Orleans with a long stopover in Nashville, or from Salt Lake City to Seattle by way of Sacramento; the mileage is about the same, but that last leg gets postponed until retirement.

Abraham's passport, had he had one to present at the Canaan border, would have listed Ur of the Chaldeans as his birthplace and Haran as a long-term residence. They were the places that first shaped him and the locations he could point to when asked that most standard of small-talk questions, "Where are you from?" But where we're *from* isn't the same as where the Lord has *brought us from,* and Abraham came to learn this. One is a matter of geography; the other, a matter of faith. One is a scattering of pins on a map; the other, a line that moves purposefully between them. Abraham (Abram then) may have been a man from Ur who'd made Haran his home for many years. But the life he'd thought settled turned out to be a stop along the route of an itinerary he never set. God transformed the pins on a map into a narrative that was still unfolding: *I am the Lord who brought you from Ur of the Chaldeans to the land of Canaan.*

The Bible's first patriarch is a towering figure in the book of Genesis, a father of faith, of covenant, and of nations. Abraham's life, his story, his devotion to God are held in highest honor. As front man in the genealogy, his name is recited in prayer ("the God of Abraham, the God of Isaac, and the God of Jacob") and recalled to memory in moments of divine address in Exodus 3 ("I AM the God of Abraham, the God of Isaac, and the God of Jacob"). He and Sarah will become progenitors of descendants as numerous as the stars, God promises. His example will inspire believers of three world religions; his flaws will inspire theological reflection on the deepest levels. But of all we could say about Abraham—and it would take years to do these texts justice—perhaps one of the most important is simply the way he and God agree upon how to tell his story: that God is the One who brought him from Ur to Canaan. That this journey was much more than a few months on the road; it would require a willingness to leave old certainties behind at every stop. That a life of faith meant trusting the itinerary to God and being ready to move, change, and change gates, when called. And that the narrative unfolding was much bigger than Abraham himself; it was about what God was doing in the world, for the world.

The long trek from Ur to Canaan is a journey we all take in the life of faith, and we come to know it well. We begin, as Abraham did, in the hometown contexts that first held and shaped us—Ur, as we've known and experienced it. We're *from* there, but we can't stay there. God and life events call, so we go forth, on the way to Canaan. And it's a very long road to get there. It's much longer than we thought. Leaving Ur, with all the change and painful growth that come with it, is much harder and more complicated than we thought. And Haran seems like it could be a nice place to stop; not exactly where we were aiming to land, but halfway, or thereabouts, and maybe far enough for now. A person can do well enough in Haran. Make peace with what is, and the way things are, and the stability of stasis: life that stays the same. Speaking and proclaiming that keep it there.

If the narrative were just about us, we could live and speak that way—for a good-enough life in a close-enough stopover—but it isn't; it's a narrative we join about the purposes of God. And to join it, we have to leave Ur and travel light. Leave old thought patterns, rooted in barrenness. Commit to the long walk toward life and justice for all God's people, with all its stops and starts and struggles to stay engaged. Listen for when the next flight is called, to "get up and go *from here*."

In Abraham, we meet a truth that often takes us by surprise: we're never too old or too settled in Haran to be interrupted again by God's call. Nothing is so fixed that it can't be reconfigured for God's purposes. Nothing is so stagnant that it can't be stirred into movement. Haran is a layover, and always was; it's a stop on the road out of Ur. And God decides when it's time for the next leg of the journey—and, for that matter, how much we can pack. Even the most enlightened of us have old certitudes that no longer fit in those carry-on bags bound for Canaan. We will *always* be repacking.

The distance from Ur to Canaan is more than eight hundred miles, over mountains and rivers and deserts and the endless stretch of our own human frailty. It's a long way to go, but an even longer way for God to bring us—from the places that formed us, through the places that need to form us still. And that's a good way to frame it when we tell the story. Wherever we started, however far we've come, God is the One who's brought us from there to here, on the Canaan road.

V

IS FOR

VASHTI

Esther 1

> On the seventh day, when the king was merry with wine, he commanded Mehuman, Biztha, Harbona, Bigtha and Abagtha, Zethar and Carkas, the seven eunuchs who attended him, to bring Queen Vashti before the king wearing the royal crown, in order to show the peoples and the officials her beauty, for she was fair to behold. But Queen Vashti refused to come at the king's command conveyed by the eunuchs. At this the king was enraged, and his anger burned within him.
>
> Esth. 1:10–12

*V*ashti makes her one and only appearance at the beginning of the book of Esther. Most lectionaries don't include her story, so many Christians have never heard of her—and maybe there are some who'd like to keep it that way. Women who wreak havoc in the empire aren't always the ones the empire remembers fondly, and women who defy their husbands aren't usually nominated for sainthood. Vashti did both. She caused an uproar with a single word, and she refused a direct order from the king himself, making every husband in the empire skittish on his own domestic front. She is the original woman who *just said no*. And even though she got the boot for it, she left the door open on her way out and provided her shoulders for the next woman to stand on. None of us can move justice forward without the example, the brave defeats, of the ones who've come before us and just said no when it counted.

Vashti's story sounds like what you might get if you crossed the Arabian Nights with *Saturday Night Live* and #MeToo: part folktale, part comedy sketch, part depressingly familiar harassment case, with a dash of palace intrigue. Her husband, King Ahasuerus, was on his 187th day of being drunk out of his mind at the party he'd been throwing for six months straight. Every official in the empire was there, along with the nobles and the army, because they'd all been invited to the royal palace in the capital city. It was meant to be the biggest party the world had ever seen, with no purpose but to feast at the king's table, drink from the king's wine, and admire the king's wealth, which was considerable. On the last night of revelry, when the guests were well into their flagons, the king decided a fitting finale would be for the men to admire his wife, too, the famously beautiful Queen Vashti. He sent word to Vashti that she was to come before them and "show her beauty"—a euphemism for wearing her crown and not much else. And she sent back word that she most emphatically would not.

The king's reaction was predictable. He was enraged and humiliated. Not only that, he was enraged and humiliated in front of all the men present, and even those not present, as the story spread across the kingdom. Women in Persia and Media heard of it. Women in Ethiopia and India learned of how Queen Vashti just said no to the king and decided they'd give it a try. Soon men who were snickering at the king in the throne room were no longer snickering. Noble ladies everywhere were discovering great potential in just saying no, as Vashti's example threatened to set off a tidal wave of rebellion. The order of the entire kingdom was disrupted. What to do?

The king, the officials, and sages put their heads together. They ask: according to the law, what is to be done to Queen Vashti because she has not performed the command of the king? They decide: let her rot. Away with Vashti and away with any woman who fails to do as her husband commands. Let another queen be chosen to take Vashti's place, and please, O Great Marduk, may her memory die with her.[1]

On one level, the men are successful. Vashti disappears, there is a cattle call for young virgins to come and compete for the queen's title, one of them is eventually crowned the new queen (see "E is for

1. Marduk is the name of the Babylonian deity.

Esther"), and as far as the church is concerned, we can get on to the real story of the book. On one level, the church has concurred with the king and his sages: it has let the memory of Vashti rot.

On another level, however, the story of Vashti cannot be erased. There are echoes of her great no reverberating all through the Bible. She lives on in the minds of her people, the king, and, most importantly, Queen Esther herself, who may never have garnered the courage she needed to speak up on behalf of the Jews of the empire were it not for her predecessor. Esther finishes what Vashti started. One injustice leads to another—but one act of resistance does too. A well-placed no can empower another person to rise up and speak out against the false rulers of this world. It can spark a whole movement. It can save an entire people.

In the Bible, there aren't many women who just say no. Quite a few of them are blamed for *not* saying no, actually (as Eve can attest), and then held responsible when their husbands don't say it either. The church has pushed it even further, with doctrine that equates sin with the failure to just say no to a snake hawking apples. But saying no to a tempting piece of forbidden fruit isn't the same as saying no to injustice and all that can follow a misapplied doctrine: sexism, misogyny, patriarchy, violence. The prophets spoke this kind of no repeatedly and relentlessly to injustice in many forms. So did Jesus. And in this chapter, so did Vashti. Refusing to participate in an act of degradation, whether inflicted on ourselves or another, unleashes a power the kings of this world will never know.

What would happen if we put the story of Vashti back into circulation? Our children could have a role model for saying no to adults who try to molest or harm them.[2] Our citizens might dare to oppose strongmen who flaunt greed and trample human rights. You and I could have a place to begin talking about the hundreds of awkward, troubling moments in our lives when our integrity is on the line, when our silence permits violence, when saying no to family and friends—maybe especially to family and friends—is the only way to

---

2. Vashti actually does get her own story, "Queen Vashti Says 'No!,'" in *Growing in God's Love: A Story Bible*, ed. Elizabeth F. Caldwell and Carol A. Wehrheim (Louisville, KY: Westminster John Knox Press, 2018), 66–67.

hold ourselves accountable to the faith we profess and the words we say we believe.

It isn't easy to be Vashti. It isn't simple and never was. But every time she says no, more space is created for the next summoning of courage, the next act of resistance.

IS FOR

WHIRLWIND

Job 40

Then the LORD answered Job out of the whirlwind:

"Gird up your loins like a man;
  I will question you, and you declare to me.
Will you even put me in the wrong?
  Will you condemn me that you may be justified?
Have you an arm like God,
  and can you thunder with a voice like his?

"Deck yourself with majesty and dignity;
  clothe yourself with glory and splendor."

Job 40:6–10

*T*he story of Job is so ancient that people have been telling it for longer than we've had Scripture in any written form. It asks the questions that human beings struggle with most: why do evil and suffering exist in this world, and what is God's place in any of it? How can a God who is good and powerful permit bad things to happen? Job doesn't come to any conclusions, because that is not in the nature of the questions: the book of Job is the puzzle that can't be solved.[1] This is probably why it draws great minds like no other book in the Bible. Artists, scholars, and thinkers the world over, religious or not, seem to feel compelled, sooner or later, to take up (or take on) Job. And since the story is so achingly familiar, it adapts, chameleonlike, to any setting.

---

1. The phrase is Kathleen O'Connor's. See *Job,* New Collegeville Bible Commentary (Collegeville, MN: Liturgical Press, 2012).

The story also brings some surprises. This book starts with a bet. Who knew that God and Satan (or *ha-satan,* "the adversary") like the occasional flutter, but apparently they do, and what they bet on is Job's endurance. God points at Job, a shining example of a man, and says, "Job is so upright and faithful he will never renounce me." Satan says, "Sure he will. Just take away everything he has." God agrees to the challenge and gives Satan free rein to prove his case, as long as he spares Job's life. Satan proceeds to kill off all of Job's considerable livestock holdings, slay his ten children, and inflict sores over Job's entire body. Health, wealth, and progeny, gone in the blink of an eye.

As Job sits down on the ash heap to mourn, his friends show up. They are very worried about him. They find his grief upsetting, his lament disturbing, and his honesty intolerable. They are quite sure Job is flirting with heresy when he bellows to the heavens, demanding an accounting from God. They are equally sure that they can explain to Job the meaning of his suffering and why he should shut up and accept it. For thirty-one chapters, they argue with him about it, back and forth, while Job shouts that he will never give up his integrity with shoddy theological explanations. And when the absurdity is so thick that even God can't stand it anymore, God shuts it down, breaking in with a whirlwind of speech and taking Job on a cosmic tour of creation. God shows Job every inch of the universe, roaring, "Where were you when I made all this? And you deign to question *me*?!"

In the end, Job relents. He confesses that there are indeed things that are beyond him, but that he is strangely comforted by the mystery of it all. God growls at the friends for not speaking rightly, as Job did, and restores everything that Job and his wife had lost: health, wealth, and more progeny. And now that everything is different, Job signals that a new order is on the way. He declares that his daughters will inherit, as well as his sons. As the cast of *Hamilton* sings, "The world turned upside down," and at the end of the book, it's true. Job is ushering in a new era for his family: new ways of sharing what we have, speaking what we know, and living with the puzzles that can't be solved.

That's the story of Job in a nutshell. And if brevity were the author's aim, it's worth noting that the story could have been told in just a few paragraphs. The book of Job could just as easily have been a two-chapter book, forty less than it is now, and as easy to fly by as some of those Minor Prophets.

But how an author chooses to tell a story is just as important as the story itself. And this author chose to include long expanses of tiresome speeches by wearisome friends who aren't *listening* to Job; they're *arguing* with him. They aren't *asking* him about his experience of grief; they're *telling* him what it should be, dictating and mansplaining with maddening certainty, on and on, for thirty-one chapters, until we want to scream—which is the author's point. Those speeches are insufferable by design. They are supposed to be so infuriating to hear that if we have to listen to *one more word* we are going to rip our hair out.

What words say and what they do are very different matters. It's one thing, as a reader of Job, to expect those speeches to be galling. It's quite another to experience them for thirty-one chapters—to physically feel the words coming at us and slamming into skin. Words that make us think, "How can Job's friends say that?! Do they not see this body right in front of them?! Does suffering render a person invisible? Or do they just not want to look?!"

What makes it worse is that the ones who are assaulting Job with these speeches aren't strangers at all, but friends. Job's friends are well-meaning people who sincerely want to save him from despair. They are trying to say the right thing in a time of trial. They are trying to comfort him—and doing a miserable job.

And *that* is something to pause over, because we know something about this, each one of us.

Job isn't just a book or some ancient myth. Job is a role, with a script that nobody wants. Yet some of us will have to play it. One day, out of the blue, that script may be thrust into our hands, along with a phone call bringing tragic news. And Job's role will be ours, for a time, however much we don't want it. The rest of us will have to take the role of Job's friends. Most of the time, that's how we enter the book: not as suffering Job, but as his devastated friends. The ones who sit with him on the ash heap for days and days. The ones who walk alongside, through the tears and the silence. The ones who try, and fail, to say the right thing. The ones who offer words of comfort, never meaning for them to be hurtful. *We are Job's friends,* trying and failing—and that is by design; it's the nature of things. Not because our words are wrong or clumsy or insensitive, but because *no* words suffice when Job sits on his ash heap to mourn. Offering words of comfort, in that moment, is utterly necessary and utterly inadequate.

But if the words of Job's friends have something important and humbling to teach us, so do Job's words, because he has things to say as well. These speeches are dialogues, and Job is bold to address his friends *and* God. He argues on two fronts. With his friends, Job laments and rages, and absolutely refuses to accept their view of his present situation. To them, he says, "My friends, you whitewash with lies. All of you are worthless physicians. Your maxims are proverbs of ashes and your defenses are defenses of clay. Until I die I will not put away my integrity from me. I hold fast my righteousness and will not let it go." On the other front, with God, Job also laments and rages and, again, absolutely refuses to accept silence from the Lord. To God, he says, "I cry to you, O Lord, and you do not answer me. I stand, and you merely look at me. I will give free utterance to my complaint. I would speak to the Almighty, and I desire to argue my case with God."[2]

Job's part of the dialogue shows us the other side of the script, words utterly necessary to say and utterly inadequate to soothe. *But they need to be spoken, and Job's friends need to hear.* Job must have freedom to voice his agony, and his friends must bear witness. It's the only way for him to make sure that nothing comes between him and his God. It's the only way for him to swoop back round to the truth he knows: his Redeemer liveth, and in his flesh, he shall see God:

> O that my words were written down!
> O that they were inscribed in a book!

---

2. Job's words to his friends: 13:4, 12; 27:5. Job's words to God: 30:20; 10:1b; 13:3.

O that with an iron pen and with lead
    they were engraved on a rock forever!
For I know that my vindicator lives,
    and that in the end he will stand upon the earth;
and after my skin has been destroyed,
    then in my flesh I shall see God,
whom I shall see on my side,
    and my eyes shall behold, and not another.
My heart faints within me!

                        19:23–27

The book of Job is the puzzle that can't be solved, but it's also the words we can never quite reach. And that is by design. We only learn it after thirty-one chapters of hanging in there, as Job's friends—or, God help us, Job. It takes that long for us to run out of words for our end of the dialogue. It takes that long for us to stop insisting that the other side make sense. And perhaps it takes that long for God to cut off the conversation with a whirlwind of things *beyond* words—God's magnificence in creation, wondrous and terrifying to behold.

From the whirlwind, we hear the dialogue that takes us into the storm and then the morning. First, God's words:

Where were you when I laid the foundation of the earth?
    Tell me, if you have understanding.
Who determined its measurements—surely you know!
    Or who stretched the line upon it?
On what were its bases sunk,
    or who laid its cornerstone
when the morning stars sang together
    and all the heavenly beings shouted for joy?

                        38:4–7

To which Job can only reply:

Therefore I have uttered what I did not understand,
    things too wonderful for me that I did not know.

                        42:3b

X

IS *IN*

AX

2 Kings 6

Now the company of prophets said to Elisha, "As you see, the place where we live under your charge is too small for us. Let us go to the Jordan, and let us collect logs there, one for each of us, and build a place there for us to live." He answered, "Do so." Then one of them said, "Please come with your servants." And he answered, "I will." So he went with them. When they came to the Jordan, they cut down trees. But as one was felling a log, his ax head fell into the water; he cried out, "Alas, master! It was borrowed." Then the man of God said, "Where did it fall?" When he showed him the place, he cut off a stick and threw it in there and made the iron float. He said, "Pick it up." So he reached out his hand and took it.

2 Kgs. 6:1–7

*S*ome stories just have the X factor, that certain something. They appeal to multiple audiences across generational and theological differences. They inspire readers from every corner to weigh in with their interpretive two cents. This little story of Elisha and the ax is a perfect example.

Elisha succeeded his mentor, the great and singular Elijah, as the next prophet in Israel. He had big shoes to fill. Once Elijah was taken up into heaven in a cinematic display of splendor—flaming chariots, angelic escorts—Elisha was left to pick up the mantle and carry on the work of his predecessor. He was certainly keen for it; he had prayed with fervor for a double portion of Elijah's spirit. But like most next-in-lines, he'd underestimated what the job would entail: political intrigue, palace drama, and exasperating power struggles within his own guild. Elisha's first few chapters as prophet in Israel are all about establishing his authority: he dashes from one miracle to the next, saving armies and villages and children from terrible fates. (He also loses patience with some boys who poke fun at his baldheadedness, and forty-two of them are subsequently mauled by bears—which qualifies less as a miracle than as a day of disaster for all concerned.[1]) Elisha is presented as both powerful and compassionate, a man who stands up to kings and cares for the lost. Even lost tools. Or so the story goes.

The company of prophets, who apparently wanted bigger and better living quarters, began a building project on the banks of the river Jordan and set about chopping down trees. One of them was so enthusiastic that he sent his ax head flying into the water, midchop. It was an unfortunate accident, but also a minor domestic catastrophe: the ax was borrowed and the young man despondent. To calm him, Elisha cut down a stick, threw it in the water, and voilà: the iron floated and bobbed to the surface. The young man retrieved his ax head and, presumably, went forth to lead a life of responsible tool ownership and meticulous maintenance.

What does the story mean? This is where the plot thickens—and curdles, in some cases. People are fascinated by this story. They find the characters compelling, the metaphors intriguing, and the fable-like quality of the tale an irresistible lure. Here's a sampling of opinions from the wide world of early childhood curricula, internet blogs, and library volumes:

> *It's a story about lost faith.* When we lose our sharp edge, when our ax heads become dull, we lose our effectiveness and the Spirit's anointing. We need to ask God for help.
>
> *It's an admonishment about pride.* When we borrow beyond our means, when we chop and build with tools that aren't ours, we're due for a fall that only God can redeem.

---

1. See 2 Kgs. 2:23–24.

It's a story about technological progress. God blesses our technological advances. When our ax heads sink, when our machines break down, they're still within God's eager reach.

It's a story about youth and age. Young people think they can do anything. But they can't, as experience inevitably shows. They need the wisdom and guidance of elders.

It's a story about the danger of disrupting sacred spaces. The Jordan River was off limits for a new building project, but the company of prophets kept testing boundaries—and losing ax heads.

It's a story that prefigures the crucifixion. The wood symbolizes the cross; the miracle of the ax's retrieval symbolizes the miracle of Jesus' resurrection. Elisha is a prototype of Christ, and the whole story points to the New Testament.

A person could despair at the wildly disparate interpretive choices, which truly seem to come from nowhere and bounce everywhere, with unabashed enthusiasm. But perhaps correct interpretation is not the point here. Maybe the point is the X factor: the fact that everyone is interested in this story and wants to participate. When we're invested, we feel free to step in and speak up. We're at the table, engaged, excited to hear what's next (how in the world can an ax head float?!). And so our conversation begins.

Yes, some biblical texts come ready-built to enthrall. Others we have to search hard to open. But the X factor is waiting to be discovered in every passage of Scripture, and we may not need to look any further than our own backyard or toolshed to find it.

Y

IS FOR

YAK

Genesis 2

> So out of the ground the LORD God formed every animal of
> the field and every bird of the air and brought them to the man
> to see what he would call them, and whatever the man called
> every living creature, that was its name.
>
> Gen. 2:19

*T*he Bible doesn't list every animal that took part in this grand naming
ceremony, but it must have been a rich array of creatures, splendid
to behold:

> Lion and puffin, muskrat and mole.
> Heron and pelican, platypus and deer.
> Turtle and sea lion, wombat and hare.
> Camel and elephant, wolf and baboon.

And the names must have been sheer pleasure to say:

> Giant armadillo and bighorn sheep.
> Southern right whale and Arctic fox.
> Red-tailed hawk and blue-tongued skink.
> Sockeye salmon and sandhill crane.

As for the naming ceremony itself, we can only guess. Maybe
the animals milled around until Adam sorted them out by genus
("*Canis* to my right, *Felis* to my left, please"). Maybe they presented

101

themselves two by two, in a precursor of boarding procedures for Noah's ark. Maybe Adam went through the letters of the alphabet as he named each creature (aardvark, badger, cougar, dolphin, egret, fisher, gazelle . . .), just for the fun of it. Or maybe he did all the As first (albatross, alligator, anteater, antelope . . .) and then the Bs and Cs and so forth, in which case the yak would have had to patiently wait its turn, squeezed in beside the yellow-bellied marmot and the yellow-billed stork—while the zebra, zorilla, and zorro brought up the rear.

We don't know the names Adam gave the creatures in this story, only that he did name them, at God's invitation and prompting. And while his creative and scientific capacities must have been in top form that day—all those great names to dream up, all those odd species to classify—something else is at work here too.

Midrashic commentary reminds us that in Genesis 2, the concept of naming is different from ours today. Naming, as Adam does it, is more than an act of imagination, or identification, or logical and scientific precision. It's an act of encounter and mutual exchange. Adam's ability to name the animals has to do with his ability to recognize their spiritual essence. To know their names means he knows *them*—and honors them. It also signals his willingness to be in relationship with them, as fellow creatures, living things who, just like him, have been created with a living soul (in Hebrew, *nephesh*).[1] They may not be partner material in the bone-of-my-bone, flesh-of-my-flesh sense. But they aren't decorative outdoor features, either: garden ornaments, say. He won't be viewing them with binoculars from afar.

Naming can have a shadow side. It can push us toward closure that cuts off future possibility by summarizing a thing or solving it or explaining the definitive interpretation by which we all must live. It can be an act of power and oppression that strips away identity—as it was for enslaved and indigenous persons who were renamed or "christened" by slaveholders or residential schoolteachers. In those cases, naming runs close to subjugation: *fill the earth and subdue*

---

1. See Ken Stone, *Reading the Hebrew Bible with Animal Studies* (Stanford, CA: Stanford University Press, 2018), 36–39.

it. And in a culture that has most often interpreted God's directive to humankind in Genesis 1:28 ("God blessed them, and God said to them, 'Be fruitful and multiply and fill the earth and subdue it and have dominion over the fish of the sea and over the birds of the air and over every living thing that moves upon the earth'") in terms of ecological domination, this shadow aspect of naming has had catastrophic consequences for the planet, for its creatures, and for us.

But naming can also be another act entirely, as it is in Genesis 2. It can signal a beginning, rather than an ending; an openness to one another, rather than a definitive line of separation. And in that spirit, this story might call us to do some soul searching of our own. What would it look like to reimagine our relationship with the earth and living things, A to Z? What would it mean to reframe it, theologically, from acts of *subduing, conquering,* and *dominating* to acts of *encountering, witnessing,* and *blessing*?

It might mean we leave room for all the animals that aren't explicitly named in this story but surely are implied. It might mean we leave room for all the encounters we haven't had yet but surely could. And it might mean we trade *itemizing* and *classifying* for *looking* and *listening;* for *meeting* and *being met;* and then for *being changed,* which surely follows.

Y is for yak. You won't find the name of that creature in Genesis 2. You won't find a yellow-bellied marmot or yellow-billed stork either. But the invitation to name them, and encounter and witness to them, is right there in verse 19—along with the alpaca, bandicoot, caribou, dingo, emu, ferret, gecko, hedgehog, ibis, jackal, kookaburra, llama, mongoose, nuthatch, ocelot, porcupine, quail, rhinoceros, seal, turkey, urial, vaquita, wallaby, xeme, yellow-cheeked chipmunk, and zokor, who are standing by. Each one with its own story and its own blessing.

Z

IS FOR

ZELOPHEHAD'S DAUGHTERS

Numbers 27

Then the daughters of Zelophehad came forward. Zelophehad was son of Hepher son of Gilead son of Machir son of Manasseh, of the clans of Manasseh, son of Joseph. The names of his daughters were Mahlah, Noah, Hoglah, Milcah, and Tirzah. They stood before Moses, Eleazar the priest, the leaders, and all the congregation, at the entrance of the tent of meeting, saying, "Our father died in the wilderness; he was not among the congregation of those who gathered themselves together against the LORD in the company of Korah but died for his own sin, and he had no sons. Why should the name of our father be taken away from his clan because he had no son? Give to us a possession among our father's brothers."

Moses brought their case before the LORD. And the LORD spoke to Moses, saying, "The daughters of Zelophehad are right in what they are saying; you shall indeed let them possess an inheritance among their father's brothers and pass the inheritance of their father on to them."

Num. 27:1–7

*T*he book of Numbers isn't exactly go-to reading for many of us. The title makes it sound like it must be about a lot of accounting, because isn't that what numbers do? They help us keep track of stuff: count it and sort it and put it in the right column, to figure out how much we have, how much we've spent, how much we owe, and how much is owed to us.

Numbers are essential if you don't want chaos. And that's really what's going on in the fourth book of the Torah: *chaos*. Rebellion, revolt, betrayal, and politics. One big crisis after another, for forty years, as the children of Israel wander through the Sinai wilderness. After the mighty acts of Exodus and the fiery words of Leviticus, what you get in the book of Numbers is the hard truth of keeping track and keeping *on* track when you're in the wilderness—which is the Hebrew name for the book, incidentally: "In the Wilderness." And when you do the numbers for a people in the wilderness, you need to be prepared for a few harsh figures.

Let's take the number of rebellions, for example. Multiple-choice question: In the forty years the children of Israel were in the wilderness, how many rebellions were there? (a) zero (b) one (c) seven (d) ten.

The answer is (d): there were ten of them—at least, as God counts them.[1] Ten rebellions—ironic, given how many commandments on stone tablets Moses has just lugged down Mount Sinai, right before the book of Numbers begins. And what were those ten rebellions about? Well, what *weren't* they about?! The children of Israel complained and whined and fussed about everything: the food and conditions, their families and leaders, how scared they were about leaving Egypt, and then in the same breath, how *mad* they were about leaving Egypt. Life there had been terrible, but at least it was familiar; and now it was over and there was no returning to it. Large numbers of the people, tens of thousands of them, got caught up in the blaming frenzy that follows too many years of too many hardships. When you can't keep faith, you keep score.

You also keep careful accounts. The children of Israel took a census when they first entered the wilderness, and they took another as they prepared to leave it, to see who among the twelve tribes was left, forty years (and ten rebellions) later. A generation had passed away in that time, but a new generation had come up, too, one that had heard the old stories and absorbed them. Among them were the daughters of Zelophehad: Mahlah, Noah, Hoglah, Milcah, and Tirzah. As Moses and the elders counted noses to know exactly how

1. See Num. 14:22–23 and God's words to Moses: "None of the people who have seen my glory and the signs that I did in Egypt and in the wilderness and yet have tested me these ten times and have not obeyed my voice shall see the land that I swore to give to their ancestors; none of those who despised me shall see it."

many men were due how many parcels of land, the daughters came forward. "Our father died in the wilderness," they said, five of them, in one voice. "He was never one of the rebels. And why should his name disappear from our family, just because he had no sons? He had us! Let us have a possession among our father's brothers."

Zelophehad was among the original company to leave Egypt, a man who had been born a slave himself. But he taught his daughters their place in the family story, that they could trace their lineage right back to Hebrew patriarchs and Egyptian nobility. Their ancestor, Manasseh, was the oldest son of Joseph and his wife, Asenath, who was the daughter of a priest of Egypt. And even though Manasseh's little brother, Ephraim, was the one who ended up receiving the blessing from Grandfather Jacob, the girls knew *that* story just seemed to happen over and over again in their family; reversal was the way of God. So were unexpected blessings. It was nothing to be frightened of, and if there were reversals up ahead that Israel hadn't imagined yet, Mahlah, Noah, Hoglah, Milcah, and Tirzah were ready. They were not about to let their family story die out simply because no one had ever thought to do things another way.

Zelophehad is an example to us. Raise children to take pride in their roots, and they will. Tell them the family stories, the range of what is humanly possible, and they will see it. Teach them the numbers that matter—ten commandments, one promise that God is with them, always—and they will value what matters: walking together on the long road to justice. Stepping up, making room, sorting through, letting go. Leaving Egypt, in every way it is possible to do that. Zelophehad did, and his daughters did too, because he taught them well. If you want liberation, teach your daughters.

Moses was taken aback when the five daughters came forward. He was the Great Liberator and Giver of the Law, the one who talked to God regularly, and even *he* had no idea this reversal might be feasible, or what he should say in response. His imagination hadn't extended as far as doing the numbers in such a radically different way. What would the outcome be? Chaos? Rebellion? More losses and grumbling? He went straight to the top to ask, which was his usual practice when he was stumped.

God is full of surprises, even for Moses, a man who thought that he'd seen and lived them all—that he and God had covered everything, when it came to rules of faith and conduct. Yet the generations rise and fall away, and new ideas emerge, new ways of counting and sorting and putting things in different columns. When we realize the numbers are off, we start again; we count on a bigger scale. We include the daughters of Zelophehad because they are indeed inheritors with us. They have a place in the land, and they are right; they *have* a right. Which is exactly what God said, when Moses went to inquire. In this family, in this land, in this book, in this heart, there will always be room. A place at the table.

New Testament

IS FOR

ALABASTER

Mark 14

While [Jesus] was at Bethany in the house of Simon the leper, as he sat at the table, a woman came with an alabaster jar of very costly ointment of nard, and she broke open the jar and poured the ointment on his head. But some were there who said to one another in anger, "Why was the ointment wasted in this way? For this ointment could have been sold for more than three hundred denarii and the money given to the poor." And they scolded her. But Jesus said, "Let her alone; why do you trouble her? She has performed a good service for me. For you always have the poor with you, and you can show kindness to them whenever you wish, but you will not always have me. She has done what she could; she has anointed my body beforehand for its burial. Truly I tell you, wherever the good news is proclaimed in the whole world, what she has done will be told in remembrance of her."

Mark 14:3–9

*M*atthew, Mark, Luke, and John are like good storytellers everywhere: they may start with the same material, but they shape it and tell it differently, with the little touches and flourishes that make each of their Gospels unique. It's not unusual for one of them to include a detail the others don't. This story about the woman who anointed Jesus is a prime example. It's in all four Gospels, with the same basic plot we read above (dinner table interruption, extravagant act, spluttering men, protective Jesus), but Mark is the only one with the nerve to let the woman make a scene *and* a mess.[1]

In Mark 14, the woman takes her alabaster jar and breaks it, right there at the table, before she pours out the oil. In fact, she smashes it to pieces; that's what the word means. It's as much commotion as if she'd walked into the dining room with an enormous jar of applesauce and flung it with great ceremony to the floor. Immediate chaos: jar shattering, broken pieces flying, shards of applesauce-coated alabaster in everyone's food. A big, sticky, splintery mess that's hideous to clean up. And while the oil in this scene would cost ten thousand times more than a forty-eight-ounce jar of applesauce—no exaggeration—the *mess* is the point, and the intentional nature of breaking open the jar. Maybe adding splatter to the splutter was a little too much for Matthew, Luke, and John, who keep the jars in their Gospels whole and intact. But Mark emphasizes the woman's act of breaking, and he wants us to reflect on it. What does it mean, to her and to Jesus, that she breaks open that alabaster jar?

A jar like this, in Jesus' day, was steeped in meaning to begin with. Alabaster is a delicate, translucent stone that was often used in antiquity for carved ornamental vases and bottles for precious oils, like the nard this one contained. An alabaster jar was expensive enough. The ointment inside was outrageous. It cost as much as a person might earn in a year, and those who could afford it saved it for their funerals. An alabaster jar of pure nard might sit on a shelf for years until it was needed to anoint a body for burial. Then it would be broken open—the jars were typically sealed—and the ointment used ceremonially. All of which is to say, this was *not* the oil for back rubs or babies or hairstyling. It was not the sort of thing a person offered around casually, as if it were a plate of hors d'oeuvres. The oil in this jar had a serious, sacred function. It wasn't to be broken into to serve the living, but the dead.

This explains why the dinner guests are so disoriented, and then shocked, and then outraged by the woman's behavior: to them, it's an ungodly scene and a mess. Who on earth takes an alabaster jar from the vault where it's supposed to sit from the day you buy it until

1. See Matt. 26:6–13; Luke 7:36–50; and John 12:1–8 for their accounts of this story.

the day you die, and then *breaks it open* before its time (a prodigal move we've seen before) and pours it all out when crashing a dinner that isn't even a funeral?!

Scholars have thought long and hard about why the woman does what she does and why it creates such a scene. Most of them conclude that she's not just making trouble. She's making good trouble, and for very good reasons.[2] Her act might be a mysterious identification ritual—anointing Jesus in the manner of kings, because she's worked out who he is, truly the Messiah. Or it might be a dangerous act of resistance—anointing Jesus in defiance of Caesar, since Roman law declared Caesar to be a god *and* king. Or it might be a prophetic act—anointing Jesus for death, because he is about to suffer and die, since this is the kind of king he is. Whatever this act is, and whatever it means, the woman isn't doing it for shock value. She's doing it out of deep conviction.

This helps us understand more about the woman's character. She is bold. And brave. And confident. And daring. And ready to risk everything. And longing to give everything. And prepared to spend everything, in one holy, extravagant gesture. And she is the only one in the room who understands who Jesus is and what that understanding requires of her, urgently, in this moment—that she anoint him with the finest oil a human being can offer up to God. What she does with this oil tells us who Jesus is.

But what she does with the jar tells us something too—about what she must do first, before she can anoint Jesus. She has to smash that jar to pieces. *Her* jar, the one with her name on it. The alabaster jar she is never supposed to open, because the oil it contains is marked for one use. It isn't an oil of life at all in that alabaster jar. It's the oil of death, her death. Stoppered up and waiting. Stuffed away in a corner, like all the other painful secrets that bleed away life.

Yet the woman takes her alabaster jar and brings it to Jesus, and she *breaks it open!*—which is the detail Mark is determined we see. He chooses the same word for "breaking open" that's used for breaking

---

2. With thanks to the late Representative John Lewis. Making "good trouble," as he put it, was a motto he lived and one he preached to graduates at many commencements, including that of my oldest son at Decatur High School in 2009.

chains and bones and, on one occasion, stone tablets (because the surprise party centerpiece that night was a golden calf). With those echoes from other stories in Scripture, we get the message loud and clear. Breaking open an alabaster jar is like smashing stone tablets over the backs of idols. Breaking chains that bind us. Crushing bones that haunt us. And it's not an accident, this kind of smashing. We need to mean it. We need to want it.

Jesus saw that the woman was breaking open her own jar of death. Offering him the oil in the purest way she knew how. He called it beautiful,[3] what she'd done—which isn't anything like what the dinner guests called it. They watched this scene unfold with something akin to horror, because to them it just looked like waste. It looked like money down the drain. It looked like a woman making trouble, with nothing good about it. And since she was an easy target and their rage was on a roll, they lit into her with relish, howling about lost hypothetical profits. All they could do was shout about how profligate she was, and how virtuous *they* would be, if they'd had charge of that alabaster jar. Why, they would have sold it! And made a sweet deal of it too! And then they'd have given the money to the poor!

Jesus had to point out that they *did* have charge of at least one alabaster jar: their own, which was probably at home in the vault. If they wanted, they could sell it and help the poor—because God knows, as long as there are men hoarding alabaster jars in vaults, there will be economic disparities that create rich and poor. That wasn't the issue here, he said. The issue was what we do with the oil that is ours and what we do when we see who Jesus truly is. Can we claim our place in the room and give with extravagant joy? Can we smash open the deathly things that hold us back? That's exactly what this woman did so beautifully, Jesus exclaimed. And from now on, you can't preach the gospel without telling her story. *What she has done will be told in memory of her.*

He might have added, "Go and do likewise." Crash a dinner. Smash a jar. Pour out all the love you have to give, and don't hold a drop of it back.

---

3. The Greek word καλὸν (*kalon*) in verse 6 can be translated "good" or "beautiful." What the New Revised Standard Version of the Bible translates as "a good service," the New International Version (among others) translates as "a beautiful thing." (NIV: "'Leave her alone,' said Jesus. 'Why are you bothering her? She has done a beautiful thing to me.'")

B

BOAT

Luke 5

Once while Jesus was standing beside the lake of Gennesaret and the crowd was pressing in on him to hear the word of God, he saw two boats there at the shore of the lake; the fishermen had gotten out of them and were washing their nets. He got into one of the boats, the one belonging to Simon, and asked him to put out a little way from the shore. Then he sat down and taught the crowds from the boat. When he had finished speaking, he said to Simon, "Put out into the deep water and let down your nets for a catch." Simon answered, "Master, we have worked all night long but have caught nothing. Yet if you say so, I will let down the nets." When they had done this, they caught so many fish that their nets were beginning to burst. So they signaled their partners in the other boat to come and help them. And they came and filled both boats, so that they began to sink. But when Simon Peter saw it, he fell down at Jesus's knees, saying, "Go away from me, Lord, for I am a sinful man!" For he and all who were with him were astounded at the catch of fish that they had taken, and so also were James and John, sons of Zebedee, who were partners with Simon. Then Jesus said to Simon, "Do not be afraid; from now on you will be catching people." When they had brought their boats to shore, they left everything and followed him.

Luke 5:1–11

*I*t was not a good morning. If fishing is your job and you've been at it all night with nothing to show for it but empty nets, when dawn comes and you pull into shore with no fish, it is *not* a good morning. You have just had what we call a lousy day at work—night, in Simon

Peter's case. For no perceivable reason. Which is frustrating, but it happens, sometimes, to fishermen and everyone else. It's like spending all day on the phone with a client and still not closing the deal. All day under the hood of the truck in the repair shop and still short three parts you need to fix it. All day with the kids in class and still it appears that none of them can do the math homework. A lousy day at work is no fun and hard to shake, especially when you know you've done everything you could, to the best of your ability, the same as you did yesterday—when you *did* close the deal and fix the truck and manage to teach the kids a little algebra. Yesterday morning after work, your nets were full. But today they're not, and who can say why? And there will be consequences. No fish means empty pockets and people going hungry—people you love. It was not a good morning for Simon Peter and his partners, and they'd been up all night, and they were tired.

Luke says Jesus was at the lake that day. *He* was having a very good morning, if the crowd is any measure; a teacher who attracts students is doing something right. And Jesus could get a crowd, even then. He hadn't been at it long—his ministry barely launched, no disciples yet—but the word was out in that region, where Jesus had been teaching in synagogues, casting out demons, and doing wondrous things. Healing people with a touch of his hands. Curing them of their diseases. He'd cured Simon Peter's mother-in-law of a high fever; Jesus had been in Simon Peter's house. He knew the fisherman, or knew who he was, which may explain why he interrupts the morning ritual of scrubbing nets to ask if he can borrow the boat.

The fishermen are at the end of their shift and perhaps their patience. They are ready to pack it in and go home. It is not an ideal time to be giving boat rides to people who don't know anything about boats or how long it takes to wash the muck out of empty nets. But Simon Peter is as well mannered as he is exhausted, and he has respect for Jesus; he's seen what the man can do. When Jesus asks, Simon Peter obliges. They get in the boat, position it just so, and Jesus holds a teaching session for the interested crowd. And when he's finished, he turns to Simon and says, "Put out into the deep water and let down your nets for a catch."

Some mechanics have a sign on the wall of their shop, a classic, that might be a joke or might not: "Labor costs: $20 an hour. $30 if you watch. $50 if you help." Simon Peter must have wished for the fisherman's equivalent. What's a carpenter's son doing telling a fisherman how to run his business? And what exactly was supposed to happen when they put out into deep water the fishermen knew well and let down their nets for fish that weren't running—just because Jesus told them to do it? And when they'd sat in the boat for a polite interval before pulling up nets Simon Peter knew would be empty, *then* what?! Would he have to find a way for the carpenter's son to save face in what was obviously going to be a fifty-bucks-an-hour job and an embarrassing situation for them both?

Whatever Simon Peter expected to happen, it wasn't what did— which was a net teeming with fish, swarming with fish. So many, the boat wouldn't hold them without sinking. So many, his partners' boat wouldn't hold them either. Andrew, James, and John were as bowled over as Simon Peter was. A day that had begun in emptiness was turning into the mighty acts of God, right here on the lake: fish out of nowhere, like manna in the wilderness. Another man might have said, "Cool!" or thanked Jesus for turning their luck around. Not Simon Peter. He got it—this abundance wasn't about profit to fill his pockets. This was a glimpse of creation as God sees it. A night of failure was breaking into a morning fresh and new as the fifth day of creation, when God made the fish to fill the seas and the fowl to fill the air, and everything was possible: abundance, plenty, and life overflowing.

Simon Peter got it. And maybe this is what Jesus had been waiting to find: disciples like Simon who recognized glory when they saw it. Twelve persons who wouldn't yawn and stretch when given a peek at the springs of the sea. Twelve persons who weren't afraid to go deep. Twelve persons who would still let down their nets when reason and experience dictated otherwise. And when those nets came up sparkling with impossible fullness, twelve persons who wouldn't pass out at the sight, but would understand what the vision was: *God's plenty for an empty world. God's creation in all its wonder.*

Simon Peter understood. He even took it like a rock—a scared rock, but a rock still worthy of the title, which is what Jesus would call him: *Peter, the rock upon which I will build my church.* Peter was the first disciple Jesus called. But first he had to calm him down. "Don't be afraid," he told the fisherman, who apparently was taking some very deep breaths. "From now on, you'll be catching people. Ready? Let's go."

Simon Peter would need what he learned that morning. Jesus wasn't calling him to a life of perennial good days, nets that are full, work that pays off. Simon Peter may not have even noticed Jesus on a day like that; he'd have had fish to sell and profits to tally. His own abundance might have been all he had room for. And who puts out into deep water *again* when they've already gone and come back, with ample success? Not the ones who've caught plenty of fish. And that night, Simon Peter hadn't. His nets were empty.

But this is the moment when Jesus appears. Maybe he knows something we don't: people who are bone-tired are in a better position to go deep. Empty nets can catch what full ones can't. And a person who's been up all night and had a lousy time of it might be too tired to argue about signs and wonders and can simply receive them— which is why Jesus was combing the beaches and the streets for his disciples, and not searching the libraries and synagogues for learned men. The kingdom of God is revealed to those broken open enough to see the tiny cracks of light. "I came," Jesus said, "to heal the sick and seek the lost, to bind up the brokenhearted and set captives free. From now on, Simon Peter, you'll be catching people, so remember what a long night on the lake is like. Come and follow me."

In April 2020, as the COVID-19 pandemic was gathering speed, the Indian writer and activist Arundhati Roy wrote a piece for *The Financial Times*. She called the pandemic a portal, a "rupture" that has forced us "to break with the past and imagine [our] world anew." We have a chance to rethink what we've done and what we've built. Historically, she says, this is what pandemics do, and

> this one is no different. It is a portal, a gateway between one world and the next.
>
> We can choose to walk through it, dragging the carcasses of our prejudice and hatred, our avarice, our data banks and dead ideas, our dead rivers and smoky skies behind us. Or we can walk through lightly, with little luggage, ready to imagine another world. And ready to fight for it.[1]

1. Arundhati Roy, "The Pandemic Is a Portal," *Financial Times* (London), April 3, 2020.

Maybe the portal is also a call. A call that comes after a long night of emptiness, failure, and painful disappointment—but that we can only hear because of those things. A call to follow Christ through a portal to imagine another world, where night breaks into a morning of fullness, a vision of creation and abundant life as God sees it.

Maybe the portal is a call, and the call a boat, for people who know how to fish at night.

C

IS FOR

CORNELIUS

Acts 10

In Caesarea there was a man named Cornelius, a centurion of the Italian Cohort, as it was called. He was a devout man who feared God with all his household; he gave alms generously to the people and prayed constantly to God. One afternoon at about three o'clock he had a vision in which he clearly saw an angel of God coming in and saying to him, "Cornelius." He stared at him in terror and said, "What is it, Lord?" He answered, "Your prayers and your alms have ascended as a memorial before God. Now send men to Joppa for a certain Simon who is called Peter." . . .

About noon the next day, as [the men] were on their journey and approaching the city, Peter went up on the roof to pray. He became hungry and wanted something to eat, and while it was being prepared he fell into a trance. He saw the heaven opened and something like a large sheet coming down, being lowered to the ground by its four corners. In it were all kinds of four-footed creatures and reptiles and birds of the air. Then he heard a voice saying, "Get up, Peter; kill and eat." But Peter said, "By no means, Lord, for I have never eaten anything that is profane or unclean." The voice said to him again, a second time, "What God has made clean, you must not call profane." This happened three times, and the thing was suddenly taken up to heaven.

Now while Peter was greatly puzzled about what to make of the vision that he had seen, suddenly the men sent by Cornelius appeared.

Acts 10:1–5, 9–17a

Cornelius shows up in the tenth chapter of the book of Acts, and he's not generally seen as the star of the show. Peter is in the spotlight at that point. And true to form, Peter is stubbornly (big surprise) clinging to his dietary practices and harboring certain prejudices against Gentiles. He's about to get his mind radically changed by a vision of a sheet, some nonkosher delicacies, and a barbecue pit— a vision that will be a turning point for him and his theology. Bracketing the vision, however, and perhaps setting the stage for it, is a little narrative about a Roman centurion named Cornelius. While Peter is dreaming about grilled pork and shellfish, Cornelius the Gentile is dreaming about *him;* he has a vision about an angel and a man called Peter, whom he has never met. The vision takes place while Cornelius is praying, and instead of dismissing it as a momentary lapse when he must have drifted off, he decides the angel meant business and he'd better take it seriously. He sends his trusted servants to invite Peter to return with them to Cornelius's house.

Peter, meanwhile, is up on the roof of his friend Simon's house, having his own out-of-body experience about exactly which animals are clean and profane ("Rise, Peter; kill and eat!"). Completely flummoxed by it, he gets another nudge from the Spirit that an entourage is on its way to him; he should greet them and be ready to travel. The next day he returns with them to Cornelius's home in Caesarea, where a bleacher full of Gentiles is waiting politely to hear what Peter has to say. Strangely moved by this warmly receptive audience, Peter realizes that what he and Cornelius have going here is definitely of the Lord's making, and who is he to refuse a bratwurst when God is buying? To celebrate, Peter preaches a glowing sermon about the Lord's impartiality toward all who believe, whether Jew or Gentile. Cornelius and his friends convert and are baptized on the spot. The chapter ends with a great outpouring of the Holy Spirit on the Gentiles and (we can surmise) a truly excellent interfaith potluck that goes on for several days. (To get the full culinary effect, read the whole chapter.)

By the time chapter 11 begins, Cornelius and Peter have parted company and the spotlight moves with Peter to Jerusalem. Cornelius will not appear again in the book of Acts, but the story of what happened at his home in Caesarea is one Peter will continue to tell, over and over, as he tries to explain his own conversion. "Once," he will say, "I thought we were God's people and the Gentiles were not. But that was before I had my dream, and my friend Cornelius had his vision, and God brought us together. And now I am sure that neither death nor life, nor angels nor religious differences, nor shrimp cocktails nor pulled pork barbecue with oysters and cheese grits on the side can separate a people from the love of God in Christ Jesus."

It's a beautiful story, a familiar story, about insiders and outsiders, *befores* and *afterwards,* and God's astonishing knack for messing with our heads: no matter what we think the game (or the menu) is about, no matter how hard and fast the rules, God likes to change things up at a moment's notice—to flick the switch on what we think qualifies as clean and profane, faithful and unfaithful, Christian and non-Christian, or wildly unexpected. God likes to do a new thing. Just to keep things lively and the people hopping, while amazing grace pours down.

Whatever Peter was expecting that day on the roof in Joppa, it wasn't Cornelius. But Cornelius was expecting *him.* Cornelius was expecting that Peter would be a person of another faith, nationality, and privilege—since Cornelius was a wealthy Roman official and Peter most certainly was not. Yet he was also expecting to give Peter his full attention, to really listen to him, across their theological and religious differences. He was willing to risk what his friends and family would think about this situation. What's more, he even invited them to come and hear Peter for themselves.

Peter preached a great sermon that day, arguably his best. It's powerful, personal, and filled with hard-won theological wisdom. He shows us what great speaking *looks* like. But Cornelius, who has no sermon of his own, shows us where great speaking *comes* from— and in this story, that's more important. Great speaking, we learn, comes from great listening. It takes a Cornelius to produce a Peter. Or rather, it takes an *encounter* with Cornelius: an encounter with the Other. What summons forth greatness in a speaker is the willingness of the Other to listen to what the speaker has to say. And that is ground we have a hand in preparing.

We're not talking about easy listening, either, in any sense of that phrase. This will be hard work, because it's listening across theological divides. It's listening past cultural differences. It's listening that refrains from snap judgments, no matter what our parents taught us. It's even listening that takes place in our own homes, while the Other, at *our* invitation, speaks freely.

Peter may have had to dig deep to talk about what happened to him, but that's only because Cornelius dug deep first. Without Cornelius, Peter would have had nothing to say and no occasion to say it. Without Cornelius, Peter's life would have unfolded very differently, and with it, perhaps the doctrine of the church.

This raises all sorts of fascinating questions. Does each of us need an encounter with Cornelius in order to speak truthfully about our own faith? Is this what we ought to be praying for—that God would send us our *own* Cornelius, someone with whom we share deep theological differences as well as overlapping dreams?

Perhaps so. Maybe we hear God best through a person we differ from most. Maybe we speak about God best when we stop aiming for the conversion of others and start listening for our own conversions. And the best part is that our Cornelius is never far away. He might live next door. She might be at the next desk. If we're ready and open to it, God may have planted a dozen Corneliuses within a mile of where we are—which means we have only to walk outside and look. Open the door and be ready for the Cornelius whom God knows *we* need to meet, and who may already be expecting us.

D

DAVID

Luke 2

And it came to pass in those days, that there went out a decree from Caesar Augustus that all the world should be taxed. (And this taxing was first made when Cyrenius was governor of Syria.) And all went to be taxed, every one into his own city. And Joseph also went up from Galilee, out of the city of Nazareth, into Judaea, unto the city of David, which is called Bethlehem; (because he was of the house and lineage of David:) To be taxed with Mary his espoused wife, being great with child. And so it was, that, while they were there, the days were accomplished that she should be delivered. And she brought forth her firstborn son, and wrapped him in swaddling clothes, and laid him in a manger; because there was no room for them in the inn.

Luke 2:1–7 KJV

*H*ouse and lineage. It's a fancy way of saying "birthplace and background" and all that goes with it. Parents and relatives. Homestead and ancestors. Family stories and family trees. What we say when the interview committee asks, "So, will you tell us a bit about yourself?"

For Joseph, *house and lineage* meant King David, his ancestor. Joseph was of the house and lineage of David, something he could say with pride. To be a direct descendent of the greatest king Israel ever had was to claim an affinity with everything David ever was. It meant you could hold your head high, even if you weren't from Jerusalem. It meant you were somebody no matter where you lived—which had to be a boost for a boy from Nazareth, a town that had heard its share of rude remarks ("Can anything good come out of Nazareth?!")[1] But Joseph had his house and lineage; he knew who he was. He knew the stories of King David and that he had a share in them. It must have given him a lot to think about as a boy, when he was learning his carpenter's trade. Did he fashion a few slingshots, just in case? Did he carve a frame for a lyre in between his other duties? Maybe he did, and maybe he even practiced his giant-killing with a few smooth stones, because a boy can dream, can't he? (See "G is for Goliath.") The distance from wood shop to palace isn't so far, about the same as the distance from shepherd to king. When a boy is from the house and lineage of David, royalty and carpentry can live under the same roof.

When Joseph grew up, when he was a man ready to get married, *house and lineage* still meant King David. But it also meant a very long trip at a most inconvenient time, for a humiliating purpose—to be counted by the emperor and taxed accordingly. Because Joseph was of the house and lineage of David, he had to walk to David's city, Bethlehem, where his ancestor David had lived. Never mind that it was eighty miles away. Never mind that his fiancée, Mary, was pregnant and in no shape to travel. Rome was all about barking orders to remind its populace who was in charge, and in conquered territories like Palestine, the decrees were often tailored to be as cruel and denigrating as possible. The emperor's tax law took special aim at Jewish identity. Jews from all over Palestine were forced to travel long distances to the cities of their ancestors, perhaps bitterly regretting they'd ever heard the names of those forebears. Joseph was one among thousands on the road, trying to keep family together and pride intact.

For Mary, *house and lineage* was what she intended to give her baby. She was not of David's line herself, but the child she was carrying would be, when Joseph raised the boy as his own. Little Jesus would be related to David through Joseph. This meant that no matter what people said, no matter how many snide comments her boy might hear about his questionable parentage, Jesus would know

---

1. See John 1:46. "Can anything good come out of Nazareth?" is what Nathanael said when Philip told him about Jesus.

where he came from—that he had literally been counted among the descendants of kings. His parents made sure of that. They went to Bethlehem for the census and delivered Jesus in David's city. They brought him to Jerusalem to be circumcised and recorded in the temple. Mary and Joseph showed their son that biology and genetics don't determine a person's lineage or their house either. It's the vows we make, the love we give, the years we put in, the distance we travel: *those* are the things that count. House and lineage require acts of intention. We claim them with pride and give them with purpose (see "G is for Growing Up").

The gospel itself is a *house and lineage,* and faith in the gospel grafts us into the family of Christ. This means that somehow we inherit all the things Jesus did, through the house and lineage of David. All the childhood dreams. All the grown-up oppressions. All the good we imagine and the struggle we encounter. All the distances we travel, from wood shop to palace, and from Nazareth to Bethlehem, on foot and a donkey's back. We inherit all that because Joseph and Mary walked long and well to give it to their son, and so to us. Those who came before them did the same. So did those who came after them. So did our own ancestors. Just to have an inheritance, a house and lineage, takes work and a lot of sacrifice, before we are even born.

As people of faith, we also inherit King David himself, just as Jesus did—and this is a more complicated legacy. David is a shining star in the pantheon of the leaders of this world, and those powers are the very ones Jesus came to shatter and transform. Jesus is *from* David's line but not *of* it. He may grow up in the full knowledge of his heritage, but he also knows he's destined to break open the presumptions that enabled it to thrive and then fall.

We might put it like this. For Jesus, *house and lineage* means reshaping his inheritance, from the kingdom of David to the kingdom of God; for us, it means paying close attention to how he does this. So we listen again to all the family stories about King David, hearing them, as Jesus did, in a new key. They show us the range and depth of what we're capable of as human beings: the shining parts and the shadows just beneath them. In those stories, David is the one who is blessed yet always falls short, who loves deeply and sins greatly, who burns for justice and then trades it for power, and cannot function without a prophet to call him out. When Mary sings of how the Mighty One has brought down the powerful from their thrones, she means David, because Jesus comes to overturn even his own house.[2]

So we listen to Jesus tell some newer family stories, too, that sit alongside the older ones from the house and lineage of David. He gives a sermon on a hillside and speaks to crowds in parables, ushering in the realm of God with sayings and stories like these. And when Jesus overturns his own house and lineage, we are part of it—the part that's being overturned. So is the church, the household of God. Our heritage is one of being constantly reframed, reformed, reshaped, and turned upside down, so that Mary's song (and Hannah's song, before her) may be fulfilled: "God has brought down the powerful from their thrones and lifted up the lowly; God has filled the hungry with good things and sent the rich away empty."

House and lineage. Yes, it's a fancy way of saying "birthplace and background," but it's also shorthand for how we manage the inheritance we're given, the house and lineage of David. It's what we have to live into, live up to, or even walk away from, if the situation requires. It's what can and must be overturned, even in ourselves. We remember that and keep our walking shoes ready, so we can go the distance when we're called. So we can walk from wood shop to stable, from cross to empty tomb, to follow Jesus along the way.

---

2. Mary's Magnificat, the song she sings in Luke 1:46–55, is modeled on Hannah's song in 1 Sam. 2:1–10.

E

IS FOR

THE ETHIOPIAN EUNUCH

Acts 8

Then an angel of the Lord said to Philip, "Get up and go toward the south to the road that goes down from Jerusalem to Gaza." (This is a wilderness road.) So he got up and went. Now there was an Ethiopian eunuch, a court official of the Candace, queen of the Ethiopians, in charge of her entire treasury. He had come to Jerusalem to worship and was returning home; seated in his chariot, he was reading the prophet Isaiah. Then the Spirit said to Philip, "Go over to this chariot and join it." So Philip ran up to it and heard him reading the prophet Isaiah. He asked, "Do you understand what you are reading?" He replied, "How can I, unless someone guides me?" And he invited Philip to get in and sit beside him. Now the passage of the scripture that he was reading was this:

> "Like a sheep he was led to the slaughter,
>   and like a lamb silent before its shearer,
>   so he does not open his mouth.
> In his humiliation justice was denied him.
>   Who can describe his generation?
>   For his life is taken away from the earth."

The eunuch asked Philip, "About whom, may I ask you, does the prophet say this, about himself or about someone else?" Then Philip began to speak, and starting with this scripture he proclaimed to him the good news about Jesus. As they were going along the road, they came to some water, and the eunuch said, "Look, here is water! What is to prevent me from being baptized?" He commanded the chariot to stop, and both of them, Philip and the eunuch, went down into the water, and

Philip baptized him. When they came up out of the water, the Spirit of the Lord snatched Philip away; the eunuch saw him no more and went on his way rejoicing. But Philip found himself at Azotus, and as he was passing through the region he proclaimed the good news to all the towns until he came to Caesarea.

Acts 8:26–40

*P*hilip wasn't one of the twelve original disciples who had traveled with Jesus and been sent out two by two. He was a deacon, chosen to be a leader in the early days of the new church when it was exploding with members and the Twelve needed emergency backup. Philip's job was to wait on tables and distribute food to widows, but he didn't get to do it for long: a wave of violence broke out against the church, Stephen was arrested and stoned to death, and for the first time the church faced the grim reality of martyrdom. The same day Stephen was killed, Saul and his soldiers started going door-to-door, searching every house in Jerusalem for Christians and dragging women and men off to prison. Those who could fled the city for their lives and scattered; Philip was among those who escaped. And with nowhere to serve in his deacon role, Philip began to sense another kind of call. He went to the city of Samaria and started preaching.

To everyone's surprise, he turned out to be good at it. Philip the deacon was a preacher. He was a man after Jesus' own heart, too, because he hadn't hesitated at all to go into non-Jewish territory like Samaria; up to this point, no one else in the church had done that. Peter, John, and the rest of the crew back at headquarters heard about Philip's success—that the Samaritans had accepted the word of God from a rookie and been baptized—and they hurried over to check, because it seemed like mission impossible to them. But the reports were true. Philip the deacon had converted a whole city of Samaritans. It was a major victory for the Christians, their first big missionary success. And who would have thought that Philip would be the preacher to accomplish it? Philip, who, if it hadn't been for Saul, would still be waiting on tables back in Jerusalem.

Philip must have been excited for his next assignment. And he must have been thrilled to see that angel of the Lord coming, with a message he could just imagine: "Your mission, Philip, should you choose to accept it, is to continue north to the biggest urban challenge yet, the city of Caesarea!" He was probably impatient to get started, too, on what he hoped would be his *second* big success story—and maybe a mention in preaching history.

Alas. Here is what the angel said: "The wilderness road from Jerusalem to Gaza. Desert. High noon. Be there."

For Philip, this had to be a blow, disappointing, discouraging, and even baffling. This angel was assigning him to a deserted stretch of road without a single village, which is not how church authorities usually respond to preachers who get results. No human being in their right mind would do such a thing—which is our cue to immediately suspect that the Spirit is involved. And to be sure, the scene that follows sounds just like a parable Jesus might have told. *The kingdom of God is like a disheartened preacher who meets an Ethiopian eunuch sitting in a chariot and reading Isaiah on a wilderness road in the middle of absolutely nowhere.*

Success is a fickle thing. We may try *not* to measure it in terms of numbers and accolades, but that's difficult to do when the culture teaches otherwise. Every day we hear that bigger is better, more is mightier. Yet the kingdom of heaven is exactly the opposite of those things—and maybe Philip needed to learn that lesson, fast. The kingdom of God is *not* like a preacher who converts an entire district, nor is it like a person who grows a faith community from zero to megachurch in an impossibly short period of time. It's like a preacher in the desert speaking to a congregation of one. Make that one a eunuch, and you have yourself a parable, which is always an occasion to learn.

The eunuch was a man of mixed power in his day: a court official of the queen of Ethiopia, important enough to be her treasurer, wealthy enough to travel by chariot, knowledgeable enough to read Hebrew, and sophisticated enough to delve into world religions. And while Ethiopians were considered the most beautiful of peoples in the ancient world, his complicated gender identity (forced castration) and the laws in Palestine concerning eunuchs (they were outcasts in every sense) placed him clearly on the outside of everything Philip was in *his* world. They were as unlikely a pair to meet and converse as we might imagine. If this wilderness road was supposed to offer

Philip preaching opportunities, the eunuch was probably the last person Philip would have chosen for his microcongregation—but then we don't always get to choose our conversation partners, do we? Sometimes they are inexplicably yet blessedly chosen for us, to help us relearn everything we know, or think we know, about success.

Philip appears to have dragged his feet for the next bit. He doesn't approach the chariot until the Spirit prods him, and he doesn't initiate conversation with the friendliest of openers. "Do you understand what you are reading?" he asks, although a more candid (and sarcastic) translation is probably "Do you *really* understand what you are reading?!" Either way, the words reveal a certain reluctance to engage, as if pieces of this scene are starting to blow his mind. And maybe that's understandable. How do we talk about matters of faith with complete strangers whose life experience is so different from our own? How do we even start? And what person hasn't wondered exactly that, when confronted with a roomful of teenagers or older persons or millennials or agnostics or parents in suburbia or men from the shelter—or worse, only *one* of any of these people? When we speak of our faith to someone, there's no place to hide. It's just a wilderness built for two, and there we are.

The eunuch could have responded to Philip's question ("Do you really understand what you are reading?!") with all manner of sarcastic retorts, but he doesn't. Instead, he throws out a question of his own: "How can I, without someone to guide me?" It's a game-changer of a word, *guide.* Not *explain* or *correct* or *enlighten,* which we might expect. In Greek, the word means *lead,* as we might do a blindfolded friend when we take them by the hand and thread them through a crowded room. In other words, the eunuch isn't asking for a lecture. He's looking for someone to walk with him as a friend. Someone to share the journey into Scripture. Someone to invite into his chariot to sit beside him—which is a perfect way to begin a conversation, and one that even Philip can learn.

So Philip the deacon climbed into the Ethiopian eunuch's chariot and sat beside him, and they read Isaiah together. Philip told his congregation of one about Jesus. He was a good preacher this time too, as it happens—so good that when the eunuch lifted up his eyes, he saw water in the desert. *Water!* And while Philip was mulling that one over, the eunuch turned to him with shining eyes and said, "What is to prevent *me* from being baptized?"—because he really did understand what he was reading. He understood it perfectly. When we have someone to guide us, sitting next to us as a friend, it's easier to believe that God's grace is poured out for us.

This is a good story to read when we need to remind ourselves what success is all about. It isn't about the accolades. It isn't about the numbers. It's about the one eunuch who is waiting for us on a wilderness road, with a chariot built for two.

F

IS FOR

FIG TREE

James 3

> No one can tame the tongue—a restless evil, full of deadly poison. With it we bless the Lord and Father, and with it we curse people, made in the likeness of God. From the same mouth comes a blessing and a curse. My brothers and sisters, this ought not to be so. Does a spring pour forth from the same opening both fresh and brackish water? Can a fig tree, my brothers and sisters, yield olives or a grapevine figs? No more can salt water yield fresh.
>
> Jas. 3:8–12

*F*ig trees are a favorite image in Scripture. We find them in parables and proverbs, stories and prophecies, all over the Bible. Their blossoms inspire love songs. Their fruit inspires visions of peace. On at least one occasion, their leaves inspire an impromptu wardrobe. And for Jesus and James, they were the perfect object lessons.

Jesus' two parables of the budding and barren fig trees are probably the best-known examples.[1] In each, he lets the botanical life cycle teach his disciples about the importance of bearing fruit in due season. "From the fig tree, learn its lesson," Jesus advises them. "Pay attention to what time it is" (Matt. 24:32–33). But in the Epistle of James, fig trees serve another instructional purpose. They aren't reminders to bear good fruit. They're reminders to speak a good word—since we're very apt to speak a grouchy one.

---

1. The parable of the Budding Fig Tree is in all three Synoptic Gospels: Matt. 24:32–35; Mark 13:28–31; and Luke 21:29–33. The parable of the Barren Fig Tree is in Luke 13:6–9.

The third chapter of the Epistle of James is about the dangers of speaking and teaching, and it reads like a Tough Love for Teachers pamphlet. The tone isn't motivational; it's cautionary. "Not many of you should become teachers, my brothers and sisters," chapter 3 begins, "for you know that we who teach will face stricter judgment" (v. 1). The problem, the author says, isn't that we might misspeak. It's that we will. The tongue is an untamable, nearly uncontrollable organ in the human body. It can blurt out words that will unleash hell. It can do more damage than a forest fire. In the same breath, with the same mouth, we speak blessings and then we speak curses—and we hardly know why, only that we shouldn't live this way, and can't stop. How we treat every person, how we speak to every person who is made in the image of God, matters. To be a blessing, we must bless.

Look to the fig tree, the author says. Fig trees produce figs, not olives. Grapevines yield grapes, not figs. If the words we say don't sound like a blessing, they aren't—no matter how we try to spin them or justify the hurt they cause. If our speaking sounds like cursing, it very likely *is*—and it's not worth opening our mouths to say any of it in the first place.

Some pulpits have a special plaque on the inside, visible only to the preacher. The words are a reminder of what the congregation is yearning for as the preacher begins to speak: "We wish to see Jesus" (John 12:21). Not all of us are preachers (and thank God for that, most of us might add), but maybe a version of that plaque would be a handy thing to keep on hand. Instead of words, it could have pictures of a fig tree, an olive tree, and a grapevine, as a last-minute check to the words that come out of our mouths and a reminder to pay attention to their yield. Then we could ask ourselves some honest questions about how we're doing.

We could ask, for instance: Are my fig trees yielding figs, so to speak? Are the words I mean as a blessing doing just that? Or have they turned into something else on the way out of my mouth, so that instead of blessing, they're doing the opposite? If that's the case, I'm a fig tree that's somehow decided to produce olives—which won't fly in the agricultural realm. I am definitely not going to score any points as a fig tree if I don't produce figs.

And what about my grapevines? Is whatever I'm saying truly helpful here, so those grapevines will give the grapes I intend? Or am I not being helpful at all and really just looking for an excuse to rant and squawk—in which case my grapevines are now as wonky as my fig trees? Look closer: are those *olives* I'm seeing, *again*—when olives were the *last* thing on my mind?! If so, my words aren't matching my actions at all, and James is going to lay it on thick: as far as he's concerned, it's time for a botanical intervention.

Of course, the people James was mostly concerned about—the ones he knew were in need of intervention, tough love, and every plaque in the store—were preachers and teachers. Those of us who answer yes to that description will have to own up: this object lesson is for us. Let's get our figs, olives, and grapevines in order.

G

IS FOR

GROWING UP

Luke 2

The child [Jesus] grew and became strong, filled with wisdom, and the favor of God was upon him.

Now every year his parents went to Jerusalem for the festival of the Passover. And when he was twelve years old, they went up as usual for the festival. When the festival was ended and they started to return, the boy Jesus stayed behind in Jerusalem, but his parents were unaware of this. Assuming that he was in the group of travelers, they went a day's journey. Then they started to look for him among their relatives and friends. When they did not find him, they returned to Jerusalem to search for him. After three days they found him in the temple, sitting among the teachers, listening to them and asking them questions. And all who heard him were amazed at his understanding and his answers. When his parents saw him they were astonished, and his mother said to him, "Child, why have you treated us like this? Your father and I have been anxiously looking for you." He said to them, "Why were you searching for me? Did you not know that I must be in my Father's house?" But they did not understand what he said to them. Then he went down with them and came to Nazareth and was obedient to them, and his mother treasured all these things in her heart.

And Jesus increased in wisdom and in years and in divine and human favor.

Luke 2:40–52

*T*he church spent a lot of years debating whether Jesus was God, man, or some combination thereof (or not). It took several centuries and four ecumenical councils for the bishops to come up with a definition most of them could live with: Jesus Christ, the Son of God, was fully human and fully divine. What that means may be simpler to express than to explain, and perhaps artists break it down for us more easily than scholars. But what it meant for Jesus' parents was that *this* boy was going to be a very interesting child to raise. Their fully human son was going to need a fully human growing up, without letting any of the son-of-God business turn his head before it was time.

Mary and Joseph didn't have bishops advising them on colic and the two natures of Christ, of course; what they knew of Jesus' cosmic identity came in fragments from different sources. They had to piece it together themselves, taking in each new revelation as it was given to them—and trying not to be so amazed that they couldn't feed and change the baby. Before Jesus was born, they'd had plenty of confirmation that God was handing them an enormous parenting task. By the time he was a toddler, Mary and Joseph had encountered a pageant's worth of characters and more news than they could absorb. They'd seen angels overhead and shepherds all over the stable. They'd opened the door to wise men with strange and expensive gifts. They'd heard prophecies from venerable elders about the extraordinary things Jesus was destined to do, using words like "salvation" and "redemption" and, most astonishing of all, "messiah."

It was good tidings of great joy, but it was a lot to hear, for first-time parents. Yet Mary and Joseph remained calm, which is nothing short of remarkable. They were a brave pair to begin with; few couples would weather conception by the Most High as gracefully as these two did. And if they didn't understand (how could they?) all the things being said about their child, they knew enough not to dismiss or disdain what they couldn't resolve. So they set it aside for later and made notes for Jesus' baby book, and Mary treasured all the words and pondered them in her heart. And maybe she hummed the words she'd said when she'd first learned that she was pregnant: her Magnificat, modeled on Hannah's ancient song.[1] Maybe that song was the lullaby Mary and Joseph sang to Jesus as he grew. If they didn't know exactly what *he* would grow to be, they did know who God was and the words to express that:

---

1. See 1 Sam. 2:1–10.

My soul magnifies the Lord,
  and my spirit rejoices in God my Savior,
for he has looked with favor on the lowliness of his servant.
  Surely from now on all generations will call me blessed,
for the Mighty One has done great things for me,
  and holy is his name;
indeed, his mercy is for those who fear him
  from generation to generation.
He has shown strength with his arm;
  he has scattered the proud in the imagination of their hearts.
He has brought down the powerful from their thrones
  and lifted up the lowly;
he has filled the hungry with good things
  and sent the rich away empty.
He has come to the aid of his child Israel,
  in remembrance of his mercy,
according to the promise he made to our ancestors,
  to Abraham and to his descendants forever.

Luke 1:46–55

We don't have any stories of Jesus' younger childhood years. After his birth narratives in Matthew and Luke, and the account of the family's flight to Egypt (see "K is for King Herod"), we skip straight to Jesus at age twelve and our story above. By this time, Mary and Joseph had settled back in Nazareth with their family. And even though we're told that "the child grew and became strong, filled with wisdom, and the favor of God was upon him," we can guess there were days when this was not much in evidence and his parents had to lay down the law. But they were prepared for that. Mary and Joseph loved their growing-in-wisdom son, and they knew a fully human boy can be a handful. So can a young messiah; they learned that too. And as Jesus grew, the complexity of their parenting task was more and more apparent. They had the usual decisions to cope with at each stage of child development (how to let him show strength with his arm, but in an age-appropriate way; how to bring down the powerful from their thrones without hitting his siblings; that sort of thing). But Jesus being the child he was, there were moments when nothing could have prepared Mary and Joseph for what they were supposed to do as parents. Adolescence, for example. What does a fully human son of God need in those years? Where will he push the limits? How will he rebel? Will he be embarrassed by his father, and which one are we talking about? Mary and Joseph had to confront questions like these that pushed their limits as parents, especially in the spring of Jesus' twelfth year.

As our story begins, they are on their way home from the family's annual Passover trip to Jerusalem. Jesus is supposed to be caravanning back to Nazareth with them, somewhere among the friends and relations. A day into the trip, his parents discover he isn't there. They begin to search for him, retracing their steps back to Jerusalem, checking at every truck stop they'd passed and every water hole where they'd fed the animals. For three days, they talk to merchants, innkeepers, bystanders, police—anyone who might have a clue about their son. But they can't find him anywhere they can think of to look. He isn't at the skate park or the video arcade. He isn't hanging out in bars, changing water into wine. He isn't in the parts of town where the hungry are filled with good things and the rich are sent away empty, and a twelve-year-old messiah might possibly be showing strength with his arm. Where else could Jesus be? Mary and Joseph are desperate.

It takes them three days of searching to find out: *their* son's idea of adolescent rebellion is to go to the temple and move in. Jesus pushes the limits by staging his own church lock-in. While he's there, he walks right up to the most powerful religious leaders of the day and starts asking questions about Scripture. Hard ones. For hours. (He is twelve, after all.) And they take him seriously, which is an unforgettable experience for a young person. They talk, and he listens. He talks, and they're amazed. They might be the same leaders who will be mad as blazes at Jesus in another twenty years. But right now, they're not mad; they're impressed. The boy has something to say. The *young man* has something to say, and it's time for him to practice saying it.

Mary and Joseph, on the other hand, are not impressed. He's their son and he's twelve, and they've just spent three days looking for him. Three agonizing days. And while they're obviously relieved, they're also furious that Jesus has put them through this. Their young rebel doesn't seem the least bit abashed or sorry either. Mary dresses him down, in front of God and everyone. If Simeon and Anna could stand up in the temple years ago and announce that her baby was destined for the rising and falling of many, she could very well do the same now and announce that his immediate destiny entailed nothing *but* falling, given his recent behavior. "Child, why have you treated us this way?" Mary exclaims. "We've been looking for you for three days, out of our minds with worry!"

Jesus remains calm. He learned that from his parents. "Why did you have to look?" he asks them, with what seems like genuine surprise. "Didn't you *know* where I'd be—here, in my Father's house?"

It might have been the moment when Mary and Joseph knew their role was changing. Jesus was growing up. He was heading into the world. And while it would be years before he left home to begin his official ministry, he was already practicing belonging to two spheres. Having parents in both. Having *work* to do in both: "my Father's business," as the King James Bible puts it. *Didn't you know I had to be about my Father's business?* When Jesus was twelve years old, the temple became the place he never wanted to leave, a second home of pure joy, where Scripture came alive and he could talk about it for hours with others who loved it as much as he did and treated him with respect. It wasn't his bar mitzvah, but it might as well have been. He was confirmed in his purpose. And since his parents had raised him to step into that purpose when the time came, he was already on the watch for it. Testing his own fullness.

The story says Mary and Joseph didn't understand Jesus' words, and maybe they *were* baffled. But they understood enough. They'd always understood enough. Raising this child was a gift and a mystery, and the best they could do was prepare his way. Help him grow up into the man he would be. Return him to God, when the time came. *My soul magnifies the Lord, and my spirit rejoices in God my Savior.*

H

IS FOR

THE HEMORRHAGING WOMAN

Mark 5

> Now there was a woman who had been suffering from hemorrhages for twelve years. She had endured much under many physicians, and had spent all that she had; and she was no better, but rather grew worse. She had heard about Jesus, and came up behind him in the crowd and touched his cloak, for she said, "If I but touch his clothes, I will be made well." Immediately her hemorrhage stopped; and she felt in her body that she was healed of her disease. Immediately aware that power had gone forth from him, Jesus turned about in the crowd and said, "Who touched my clothes?" And his disciples said to him, "You see the crowd pressing in on you; how can you say, 'Who touched me?'" He looked all around to see who had done it. But the woman, knowing what had happened to her, came in fear and trembling, fell down before him, and told him the whole truth. He said to her, "Daughter, your faith has made you well; go in peace, and be healed of your disease."
>
> Mark 5:25–34 NRSV

*S*he was a woman who had been suffering from hemorrhages for twelve years. When did she finally name that for herself? Human beings are not always as forthcoming and honest about our own pain as it might behoove us to be. We can go along for years, making excuses. What's a little blood and a little pain? Nothing we can't handle, when life is busy and we have things to do, and so many other people are bleeding a lot worse than we are. But the weeks go by, the months lengthen, and every morning, there it is again, a little blood and a little pain. Each day a little worse. And when do we finally cross the line to that word "hemorrhage"—bleeding that doesn't stop? When is the moment we realize we're in over our heads? A hemorrhage takes over. It can take over a person's identity, as it did for this woman. We don't even know her name; Mark just calls her the hemorrhaging woman. The woman who had been taken over by suffering. And when did she finally realize and name this for herself? After twelve years of denial? Twelve years of physicians? Twelve years of crushing treatments and expenditures? All we know is she'd spent all that she had, in every sense, and "she was no better, but rather grew worse."

But she had heard about Jesus. What had she heard? It must have been something incredible. And to be sure, there were plenty of incredible stories in the air; people were saying all sorts of things about Jesus:

> We've found him, the one whom Moses and the prophets wrote about! (John 1:45b)
> Come, see a man who told me everything I have ever done! He can't be the Messiah, can he? (John 4:29)
> What is this? A new teaching—with authority! (Mark 1:27b)
> He commands the unclean spirits and out they come! (Luke 4:36b)
> A great prophet has risen among us! (Luke 7:16b)
> What sort of man is this, that even the winds and the sea obey him? (Matt. 8:27b)

The streets were buzzing with such reports and excitement about Jesus. People were saying extraordinary things. They were linking him with Elijah and the Most High God and the words of the prophets. They were going back over Scripture they knew by heart, had heard a thousand times, and they were making connections:

> Have you not known? Have you not heard?
> The LORD is the everlasting God,
>   the Creator of the ends of the earth.
> He does not faint or grow weary;
>   his understanding is unsearchable.
> He gives power to the faint
>   and strengthens the powerless.

Even youths will faint and be weary,
  and the young will fall exhausted,
but those who wait for the LORD shall renew their strength;
  they shall mount up with wings like eagles;
they shall run and not be weary;
  they shall walk and not faint.

Isa. 40:28–31

His fame was spreading, the crowds were gathering, and he'd even been called the Holy One of God. Extraordinary things, and the woman heard. She heard what the people were saying about Jesus. She said to herself, "If I only touch his *clothes,* I will be made well!" so she slipped into the crowd and she did.

Jesus felt the power go out of him immediately, just as the woman felt in her body that she was healed. "Who touched my clothes?" he asked, and the woman fell down at his feet. She didn't just tell him the truth. She told him the *whole* truth, something much harder—so hard, in fact, that she is the only person in the Gospels to have done so. She told Jesus that she was a woman taken over by suffering whose life was bleeding out of her, but that she'd heard about him and what he could do. She'd heard that he could heal her with a single touch, and she'd believed it, what people were saying about Jesus. That was the whole truth. And she told it on her knees, for everyone to hear.

Jesus made sure they did. He blessed her and called her "daughter." He said, "Your faith has made you well." He said, "Go in peace," so the crowd would know they had a role here, too, which was to *keep* the peace. Welcome her among them; no questions, no quarrel. She was a child of God, not a nameless hemorrhaging person, and Jesus made sure they all heard it.

What have we heard about Jesus? It's important to ask. Because what we've heard may become what we say and then what someone else hears—or overhears. And we never know, we *never* know, who may be listening, and spent, and weary, and longing to rise up. Longing to hear incredible things. *They shall run and not be weary. They shall walk and not faint.*

I

IS FOR

INDIA

John 20

When it was evening on that day, the first day of the week, and the doors were locked where the disciples were, for fear of the Jews, Jesus came and stood among them and said, "Peace be with you." After he said this, he showed them his hands and his side. Then the disciples rejoiced when they saw the Lord. . . .

But Thomas (who was called the Twin), one of the twelve, was not with them when Jesus came. So the other disciples told him, "We have seen the Lord." But he said to them, "Unless I see the mark of the nails in his hands and put my finger in the mark of the nails and my hand in his side, I will not believe."

A week later his disciples were again in the house, and Thomas was with them. Although the doors were shut, Jesus came and stood among them and said, "Peace be with you." Then he said to Thomas, "Put your finger here and see my hands. Reach out your hand and put it in my side. Do not doubt but believe." Thomas answered him, "My Lord and my God!" Jesus said to him, "Have you believed because you have seen me? Blessed are those who have not seen and yet have come to believe."

John 20:19–20, 24–29

*L*egend and tradition have it that India is where the apostle Thomas landed, in 52 CE. While Paul was busy in Greece and Asia Minor, Thomas quietly set sail for points east, came to Kerala, on India's southwest coast, and founded a church that flourished for fifteen centuries before anyone back home knew a thing about it. When Portuguese missionaries arrived in Goa in the early sixteenth century, intent on converting the populace, imagine their surprise when they were met by faithful Christians who had functioned perfectly well for more than a millennium without benefit of pope, patriarch, or Scripture.[1]

The story of Thomas in India isn't recorded in our Bible. You won't read about it in the book of Acts, and there are no epistles to the church in Kerala tucked between the letters to the Philippians and the Colossians. What you *will* read is that Thomas is the disciple who doubted Jesus' resurrection. You'll read it every year if you follow the lectionary; Doubting Thomas makes his traditional appearance a week or two after Easter in the assigned John 20 text. It's his fifteen minutes of fame, biblically speaking—but it's not the whole story. As the church in India will attest, there are other ways to look at Thomas, because even Scripture can't capture all there is to see and say about the Word of God alive in the world.

We first see Thomas when he's called to be one of the Twelve, one of Jesus' disciples. True, he's not the flashiest of them. He doesn't leap out of boats or walk on water or argue about whether he'll sit at Jesus' right or left hand. He doesn't get a starring role at the Last Supper, like Peter and Judas, or recurring cameos, like James and John. Thomas's distinguishing features are that he asks good questions and has a twin sibling, somewhere; locally, he's known as Thomas the Twin. It's a good nickname and one he might have kept if it weren't for the twentieth chapter of John. Up to this point in the Gospels, what we know of Thomas is that he's a steady disciple, reliable, competent, content with his supporting role. He's doing his job, which is to show up and be an eyewitness to the life and ministry of Jesus. Until the key moment comes, the moment of resurrection, and he misses it.

1. The Mar Thoma Syrian Church of Malabar (or Mar Thoma Church), one of the oldest Christian denominations, is believed to have been founded in 52 CE by the apostle Thomas in Kerala, India. It has more than a million members worldwide. The church describes itself as "Apostolic in origin, Universal in nature, Biblical in faith, Evangelical in principle, Ecumenical in outlook, Oriental in worship, Democratic in function, and Episcopal in character" (https://marthoma.in).

He misses it. The risen Christ appears to the disciples in the middle of a locked room, and Thomas, for the first time, isn't there. What's more, he's the only one absent. It is the absolute worst moment to be late, or stuck in traffic, or out for air, or simply the guy who was sent to pick up the pizza, but that's how resurrection unfolds in the Easter stories. Some see it and some don't. Some are there and some aren't. Some happen to be at the tomb or on the road to Emmaus or huddled together in a house, and others, for reasons too mundane to pick apart, aren't, and so they miss it; they miss the risen Christ. It isn't their fault—or at least, the text doesn't assign blame along those lines. But it does present an equal opportunity challenge. When resurrection happens, when some of us are eyewitnesses and others aren't, how do we speak to one another of what we've seen and what we haven't seen?

Both experiences are important, and they require a lot of practice. The Easter stories provide exactly that: space for Jesus' disciples and followers to practice the gift of seeing what God is doing among us as well as the gift of *not* being the ones who see—and who therefore must hear about it secondhand. In both cases there's a lot of fumbling around, because no one does it perfectly the first time. To wrap your head around resurrection, whether you're seeing it with your own eyes or hearing about it from your best friend, requires an imaginative fortitude that wildly exceeds the average daily allotment.

Thomas fails at this the first time around. It isn't that he can't believe what he hears, it's that he won't. He won't believe unless he sees for himself. This is an impressive demonstration of how the ego, when threatened, can turn on the imagination and squash it. ("Resurrection?! How come *I* didn't see that?!") So rather than rejoicing at what God is doing in the risen Jesus, Thomas explodes in conditional statements that change the subject from God to himself: "Unless I see the marks of the nails in his hands, and put my fingers in his side, I will not believe!" he declares to the rest of the disciples.

Thomas sounds a bit like a frustrated toddler here. He might as well have folded his arms and stomped his foot, and perhaps he did. To be a secondhand witness to resurrection requires, first and foremost, a resolve not to take it personally that *you weren't there.* It demands an imaginative maturity to remember that this is not about you; this is about what God is doing to reconcile our broken world. This is about God's decisive no! to the powers of death, rather than God's decision to perform miracles in your presence or absence. And in this moment, at least, that kind of imaginative maturity eludes Thomas.

Jesus is charitable in referring to Thomas's outburst as a moment of doubt rather than a temper tantrum. He allows Thomas to fulfill his conditional demands—to place his fingers in the marks of the nails—and then invites Thomas to rethink the whole situation. What was this about, really? Was it about the fact that resurrection is so impossible to believe, or that everyone else saw it and Thomas didn't? Was it about believing or doubting that the witness of others might be true, or putting God to the resurrection test—another version of "Come down from the cross, and we'll believe"? Was God the subject here? Or were you, Thomas?

Common wisdom has it that doubt is the opposite of faith, but perhaps this isn't quite accurate. In Thomas's story, doubt is the warping of the faithful imagination: the inability to change the subject from ourselves to God. Doubting is insisting on seeing and experiencing resurrection in the same way that others have—and blaming God when this doesn't happen. Doubting is making conditional statements that limit God's activity within certain prescribed barriers. Doubting is encircling the human imagination and giving the ego free rein: if we don't see it, we won't believe it. It isn't that we *can't*. We *won't*.

Changing the subject, however, is something else entirely. It's setting sail for India, so to speak—going places near and far that no one back home has even imagined existed. It's leaving old maps and borders behind and replacing them with partnerships. It's sharing gospel with people who hear and absorb it into their own culture. It's caring less about whether your name goes down in the annals of glory for what *you* did, and more about whether God's glory continues to rise in places you'll never see.

Whatever Doubting Thomas had to learn, he did it well. The next we hear of him, it's fifteen centuries later, which sure puts things in perspective for those of us who worry about whether what we do will have any lasting effect after we're gone. *You never know.* Even the most egocentric, imagination-deprived among us can have a change of heart and a change of subject. Even the most pot-bound among us can be transplanted from Galilee to India.

Maybe that's why Thomas's story comes up every year: we need constant reminding that resurrection isn't about us and what we're doing. It's about God and what God is doing. So be open. Be patient. Cultivate an apostolic imagination, and let it carry you somewhere that isn't even on your map.

J

IS FOR

JOHN THE BAPTIZER

Matthew 11

> When John heard in prison what the Messiah was doing, he sent
> word by his disciples and said to him, "Are you the one who is
> to come, or are we to wait for another?" Jesus answered them,
> "Go and tell John what you hear and see: the blind receive their
> sight, the lame walk, those with a skin disease are cleansed, the
> deaf hear, the dead are raised, and the poor have good news
> brought to them. And blessed is anyone who takes no offense
> at me."
>
> Matt. 11:2–6

*J*esus didn't go over the top with praise for many people, but he did
for his cousin John. "Truly I tell you, among those born of women
no one has arisen greater than John the Baptist!" he declared (v. 11).
He meant it too. John, resplendent in camel's hair, was the king of
prophets, and the person and preacher that Jesus admired most.

Jesus and John were relatives, but their affinity went far beyond
that. They were as closely aligned as the prophecies about them:
Jesus was the Messiah and John was the one sent to prepare his way.
Jesus was Lord and John was his prophet. Jesus was the way and
John made the path straight. They even knew one another in utero:
John's mother, Elizabeth, exclaimed that the baby within her leaped
with joy when the newly pregnant Mary came to visit. When they
grew up and began their ministries, Jesus came to John to be baptized, because that was the proper thing, he said; it was the way to
fulfill all righteousness. Jesus' confidence in John, his conviction

149

that John was the Elijah who is to come, helped him to step into his own role when the time came. You have to hand it to divine wisdom: what better way to prepare a messiah for what's coming than by having his own cousin walk a few lengths ahead?

Here's something else John prepared Jesus for: the moment when everything you're sure of dissolves. *Are you the one who is to come, or are we to wait for another?*

John asked Jesus this question only months after shouting to all who would listen that Jesus *was* the one. It's such a shock to read his about-face that at first, you might think you've gotten the name wrong. *John?* The man who proclaimed to thousands that the kingdom of heaven was at hand? The man who pointed straight at Jesus and said, "Behold the Lamb of God"? The man who, more than any other, was born and raised to preach the realm of God with absolute certainty?

You really might think you've gotten the wrong name, or at least the wrong John, since this question seems to belong on the lips of somebody else—one of the ever-bumbling-and-stumbling disciples, for example. Peter, James, and John are frequently involved in episodes of messianic identity and misidentity. They seem like perfect candidates for this question. But the mighty Baptizer? It's difficult not to be caught off guard on that one. It may have been difficult for Jesus too. John was supposed to be the voice crying in the wilderness, not the voice wondering in the wilderness. *Are you the one who is to come, or are we to wait for another?*

Context matters, of course. John didn't just get up one morning, eat his eggs and locusts, and take a hairpin turn into uncertainty. He was in jail, in King Herod's palace, and he'd been there for some time. He was waiting to hear how the king was going to punish him for preaching a few sermons on royal family values that hadn't gone over well. And while he was waiting, he'd had time to think about things: how he'd spent his life, and the kingdom he'd preached, and the person he'd proclaimed, and whether any of it had actually come to pass as he'd said it would.

John decided that from where he was sitting, the world didn't look any more redeemed than it had when he'd first gone to the desert to start his ministry. The crooked paths weren't any straighter. The rough places weren't any smoother. The mountains and valleys were just as high and low as they'd always been; nothing had been filled in or made low, as Isaiah promised it would. No one was sharing what they had or bearing fruit worthy of repentance, and the only ax lying about was in the hands of Herod's court executioner—who probably had other things in mind for it than chopping down trees.[1] If the Messiah had come and made any difference at all, John couldn't see it. All he could see was that Herod and Caesar were still on their thrones doing just as they pleased, and God's prophets didn't stand a chance against them.

Disillusionment is a terrible thing, and no person of faith is exempt. Not even John could avoid it when his turn came. A disillusioned person looks out at the world and sees only bitterness. Justice shredded. Hope splintered. God inexplicably absent. It isn't necessarily the way things are, but it's the way things seem. It's the view from captivity. We find ourselves staring through that kind of half-light whenever we, like John, are closed in, cut off, fed up, or bowed down by all we cannot change in this world.

A disillusioned person isn't sure anymore. The bitterness is corrosive; it eats away at what we thought we knew. It gnaws on foundations we thought were firm. We start to form questions that days ago would have been unthinkable: *Are you the one who is to come, or are we to wait for another?* We think seriously about changing direction and even allegiances. In the half-light, everything is perilous and nothing is clear.

John is not the first disillusioned person of faith to come around in Scripture—Elijah and Jeremiah would attest to that—but he's certainly one of the most courageous in the moment. Sitting at the bottom of his prison cell with the world closing in on him, he could have chosen to go down into silence, but he didn't. He spoke up. He spoke out—not to the crowds, this time, but to Jesus, sending word through

---

1. See Matt. 3:10 for the excerpt from John's sermon: "Even now the ax is lying at the root of the trees; therefore every tree that does not bear good fruit will be cut down and thrown into the fire."

his own disciples. He voiced the question that had been haunting him, believing it worthy of respect. He asked for direct confirmation. And he indicated his readiness to settle down and wait for an answer, even if it meant an overhaul in divine personnel. John stood up and reached out to his Lord, expecting to be addressed in return. Sometimes that's the bravest thing a person can do.

Jesus understood the context behind John's question. He knew that his cousin was speaking from a place of deep containment, in every sense of that word, and that it wasn't the time to rebuke him ("Get behind me, Baptist!") or shame him ("How can you, of all people, ask me that?!") with some sort of family guilt trip. Instead, he responded with a simple description of the world outside John's cell. "Go and tell John what you hear and see," he told John's disciples, "the blind receive their sight, the lame walk, those with a skin disease are cleansed, the deaf hear, the dead are raised, and the poor have good news brought to them. And blessed is anyone who takes no offense at me." He might as well have said, *Tell John that the kingdom he preached is still at hand, and God, in God's wisdom, is still at work. Tell John that he isn't forsaken, and his life and ministry mean something. They mean something, and everything, to me.*

There are scholars who inform us that the significance of this moment in John's imprisonment is mainly that it foreshadows Jesus' own, and they have a point. Like John, Jesus will eventually be arrested and executed too. The cousins share a similar fate, and it's true that John prepares a certain path for Jesus to walk. But it's also true that John prepares Jesus for a certain reality: the time will come when Jesus, too, questions his life and ministry, and even his God. The work of proclaiming the kingdom includes the work of struggling to see it, and sometimes—from the depths of a cell, from the height of a cross—it seems nearly impossible.

So what do we do when it's our turn to question our own life and faith? What do we do in our own seasons of deep containment? We do what John did. We speak up. We speak out—and to Jesus, directly. We voice the questions that have been haunting us, believing them worthy of respect. We expect to be addressed in return, because as the mighty Baptizer shows us, a person of faith never goes down into silence. A person of faith goes straight to the source of all life and waits for the word that will come.

And if we can't yet say it ourselves, we ask someone we love to tell us what they hear and see, until we can hear it and see it again for ourselves—and begin to believe it again: *The kingdom John preached is still at hand, and God, in God's wisdom, is still at work. You are not forsaken. Your life and work mean something. They mean something, and everything, to me.*

K

KING HEROD

Matthew 2

When Herod saw that he had been tricked by the magi, he was
infuriated, and he sent and killed all the children in and around
Bethlehem who were two years old or under, according to the
time that he had learned from the magi. Then what had been
spoken through the prophet Jeremiah was fulfilled:

"A voice was heard in Ramah,
    wailing and loud lamentation,
Rachel weeping for her children;
    she refused to be consoled, because they are no more."

Matt. 2:16–18

*G*od's liberators never come into the world in peace. Moses had
Pharaoh. Jesus had Herod. The extravagant violence, the atrocious
arrogance, of these rulers is shocking. So is the body count, which is
a direct response to perceived insubordination. When Pharaoh saw
he'd been tricked by the midwives (who said the Hebrew women
were vigorous), when Herod saw he'd been tricked by the wise men
(who went home by another way), both men reacted with explosive
rage. They ordered the mass killing of infants and children—to elim-
inate threats to national security, they claimed. But being duped in
their own throne rooms was probably the catalyst. Rulers who think
they've been made a fool of are the most dangerous threats of all (see
"P is for Puah").

In the end, however, as we know, they didn't succeed: baby Moses
and baby Jesus were saved. Moses' mother built a little ark. Jesus'

father had a dream. The children were spirited away to safety and went on to grow up into the roles they were destined to take. It might well have gone otherwise, as it did for all the other families. But Moses and Jesus were spared. And a shadow of death will always fall across their stories of rescue and survival as infants, because of the bloodshed that erupted around them (see "D is for Deliverance").

Some stories in the Bible are hard to read but are given to us to tell all the same. We tell them to keep from forgetting, because selective amnesia is one of the things mortals are best at. It's why the National Memorial for Peace and Justice in Alabama, the Canadian Museum for Human Rights in Winnipeg, the US Holocaust Memorial Museum in Washington, DC, and similar places were created: to remember, with fierce resolve. To mourn. To reflect at the deepest levels. To insist that the truth is told. To honor. To pray. When we visit these places, we are changed. We aren't bystanders anymore, if we ever were, and we can never be that again. We are witnesses, and it remains for us to decide what kind of witnesses we will be. This story in Matthew is a similar kind of place. It's a text of terror and an account of murder—and lest we forget, it's been given to us to tell. Not to explain or cover or justify or defend. Simply to tell, with as little embroidery as possible, so the truth can do its own work.

Jesus would have known this story. As he got older, his parents must have given it to him to tell and know for himself—that once, he'd been a refugee in Egypt, because it wasn't safe for him in Israel. Like Moses, Jesus spent a good part of his growing-up years in the in-between spaces. It must have made him sensitive to what an outsider feels. It must have helped him understand what an immigrant faces daily. And it must have underscored what a gift his life was and how that gift could never be taken for granted. Other families in Bethlehem had suffered terribly when he was born, with no angels to warn them about any of it. Jesus was painfully, inextricably linked to those slaughtered innocents. He was a survivor of terror and violence.

Once every three years, the lectionary hands us this story in Matthew on the Sunday after Christmas. But what would it be like to tell it *every* year—to sit down together on the last Sunday of the calendar year and quietly read it aloud? What would it be like to remember those who have died in the name of Jesus, those who have died in the name of the God they worship, those who have died under conditions of terror and violence, those who have died in the cause of liberation? What would it be like to covenant together, every Christmas season, to remember?[1]

We won't know the names of every person who has died, but we will know some. And as the Black Lives Matter and Say Her Name movements have shown, it is powerful and essential work to say the names, aloud and again. Say their names, learn what we can of their stories, and work to change all that permitted and even sanctioned their deaths. Join with others who are lifting up more names every day in acts of protest and faith. This is work the church at its best has always done as a part of its mission. Remembering the martyrs and recounting their stories—including this story in Matthew 2— inspires us to be instruments of peace.

---

1. We can get some help in this if we follow the sanctoral cycle, which is the list of saints' feast days for each date of the calendar year. Stephen, the first martyr of the church, is given December 26. John the Evangelist, who told of the incarnation, is given December 27. And the children slaughtered in Bethlehem, who were martyred *because* of Jesus' birth, have the third most honored place for saints: Holy Innocents Day is December 28.

L

IS FOR

LAODICEA

Revelation 3

> I know your works; you are neither cold nor hot. I wish that
> you were either cold or hot. So, because you are lukewarm and
> neither cold nor hot, I am about to spit you out of my mouth.
>
> Rev. 3:15–16

*I*n the big wide world of aspirational adjectives, "lukewarm" doesn't
usually make the cut. Social awareness campaigns don't encourage
girls to be bold, confident, fearless leaders by launching #Lukewarm-
LikeAGirl initiatives. The military doesn't recruit soldiers with slo-
gans like "Be All That You Can Be: Lukewarm." Preachers don't send
their flocks out the door with the charge "Finally, beloved, whatever
is true, whatever is honorable, whatever is just, whatever is pure,
whatever is lukewarm, think about these things." The truth is that
unless you're a bottle of baby formula, or yeast activating in water,
lukewarm is the last thing you want to be—unless *tepid, halfhearted,
indifferent,* and *unenthusiastic* appeal to you, and seem like adjectives
you'd choose to brighten up a résumé or online dating profile.

And here we have an excellent case study of how imagery works
in context. *Lukewarm* may be an undesirable descriptor for us, but in
Laodicea, it conjured very different associations. Laodicea was a city
on the river Lycus in Phrygia, home to one of the seven churches of
Asia mentioned in the book of Revelation. The city had wealth and
sophistication, thriving commerce and every luxury, but a serious
water problem, including a lack of drinking water. A splendid aqueduct was built to pump water from neighboring towns to address the

problem: hot mineral springs through one set of pipes, cold mountain springs through another. But by the time the water reached Laodicea, it was no longer hot or cold. It was lukewarm and calcified from its journey through the pipes. It wasn't refreshing to drink or even fit to drink, and certainly not restorative. No, it was water that made you want to gag, like reaching for a mug of steaming hot coffee or a bottle of your favorite iced soft drink and discovering on first gulp that it's been sitting out for hours, room temperature and flat, with a strange aftertaste of . . . chalk.

To the citizens of Laodicea, *lukewarm* wasn't just another term for ambivalence. The very word made them want to spit, or worse; it described the bilge they got every time they opened the taps. What better way to get the attention of the church in Laodicea but to take their least favorite adjective, the one guaranteed to provoke an immediate physical reaction, and put it on the lips of the Lamb of God?

It takes a writer of exceptional skill and prowess to use imagery as the author of the book of Revelation does:

> Seven stars, seven lampstands, seven seals, seven bowls.
> Angels and dragons, thrones and beasts, horses and riders, Alpha and Omega.
> The lake of fire and the marriage supper of the Lamb.
> A new heaven and a new earth: the jeweled city of God.

And words as beautiful as these are rare in the writings of this world:

> Then the angel showed me the river of the water of life, bright as crystal, flowing from the throne of God and of the Lamb through the middle of the street of the city. On either side of the river is the tree of life with its twelve kinds of fruit, producing its fruit each month, and the leaves of the tree are for the healing of the nations. Nothing accursed will be found there any more. But the throne of God and of the Lamb will be in it, and his servants will worship him; they will see his face, and his name will be on their foreheads. And there will be no more night; they need no light of lamp or sun, for the Lord God will be their light, and they will reign forever and ever. (22:1–5)

The writing is pure genius, and so is the use of imagery. It stirs and moves and enthralls and terrifies us, all at the same time. It also uncovers truth, which is what apocalyptic writing aims to do, and what "apocalypse" means, in its original sense: an unveiling. A revealing. A disclosing of what has long been hidden. No matter how discomfiting or shocking or objectionable that truth might be: apocalyptic aims to inflame.

We can only imagine that the members of the church in Laodicea experienced a fair amount of discomfiture and shock when they heard the book for the first time. The same might go for the churches in Ephesus, Smyrna, Pergamum, Thyatira, Sardis, and Philadelphia, because the text has choice words for each. But the author saved the best and wickedest imagery for last, as writers often do. And we can only hope that the church in Laodicea heard it in the end— that their riches and privilege and allegiance to empire values were corroding the gospel. Their church was like water traveling through chalk-encrusted pipes, not fit to drink. And they needed to pay serious attention to it, the author warned, because at the moment, they were seriously compromised. Jesus himself found them as vomit-inducing as their own city water: they were *lukewarm*. The word must have generated a great, collective cringe.

The imagery we use has the power to unveil truth, often with more expedience and efficiency than plain words or speech. And those images change from context to context. Words that evoke a shudder in one place, drawing on a collective memory of some painful or joyful experience, may elicit no reaction whatsoever in another. Or they may be misconstrued and drained of their original power, which is precisely what has happened with this *lukewarm* image. Readers today could easily assume that this text means to be a corrective for widespread apathy or lackluster faith—but that's not it exactly. Christ isn't reminding us to be enthusiastic for the gospel. He's pleading with us not to corrode it. And the author of the text is counting on the Laodicean communal consciousness (and gag reflex) to do its work: "Are we so dazzled by wealth, so captive to its pursuit, that we can no longer be a conduit for God's justice? Have we become as lukewarm and contaminated as our city water supply? Or God help us: have we built a church as malfunctioning and ill conceived as our state-of-the-art imperial aqueduct, the pride of Rome and a misery to us who live here?"

Speaking and proclaiming in an apocalyptic mode has always gained momentum from wild and woolly imagery. But maybe it works best with home-grown images. When we have a hard word to speak—an unveiling, uncovering word—what would it mean for us to search our shared memory and experience for the images that already speak loudly in our communities?

> To you, the churches in hurricane-threatened coastal areas: you have become highways that lead in only one direction—away from the storm. Why are you abandoning those left behind in the hurricane's path?
>
> And you, the churches in water-parched desert cities: you are empty reservoirs who have been drained too quickly and for frivolous reasons. Why are you wasting precious water to grow grass lawns in desert soil?
>
> And you, the churches along great rivers: you are the cities upstream who consume so much water that nothing is left for those down the river. Why do you feel entitled to take more than your share?
>
> And you, the churches in glacial mountains and geothermal pools: you are hidden hot springs known only to locals. Why have you turned inward and jealously guarded the grace that belongs to all?
>
> And you, the churches in industrial cities: you are lead pipes running under the city, slowly poisoning the drinking water of children and the poor. Why do you tell lies to protect your name and sacrifice the most vulnerable among us?

These are words of judgment, revealing harsh truths. But we Laodiceans need to hear them, loud and clear. Before any of us can enter the jeweled city of God, we have to tend to what is most wretched in us—pitiable and poor, as the text puts it. Only then will we know the riches Christ offers: gold refined by fire, anything but lukewarm.

M

IS FOR

MARY MAGDALENE

John 20

> But Mary stood weeping outside the tomb. As she wept, she
> bent over to look into the tomb, and she saw two angels in white
> sitting where the body of Jesus had been lying, one at the head
> and the other at the feet. They said to her, "Woman, why are
> you weeping?" She said to them, "They have taken away my
> Lord, and I do not know where they have laid him."
>
> John 20:11–13

*P*reaching isn't something most people sign up to do. That's not surprising, given how the word is usually defined ("delivering a religious talk or sermon," "offering opinions on morality in order to persuade others," and "doing this in a really annoying and boring way"). A more useful definition of preaching might simply be *announcing,* and in Christian contexts, that means announcing the good news of the gospel. It's a form of proclamation that's open to anyone and everyone, not just the professionals—which means we may not always recognize the preacher right in front of us, not at first. Sometimes preachers hide. They're the unexpected characters in the corners and at the edges, disguised to make us think they aren't preachers at all. Even in Scripture. Especially in Scripture. But if we look closely, if we listen closely, we'll find them, announcing a word that was meant for us. This story in John's Gospel may be the best example of that, because Mary Magdalene, it must be said, sets the bar.

Mary's not the first person you think of, when you think of a great preacher. She didn't have a pulpit or a congregation or a lot of degrees to indicate her splendid homiletical education. Mary wasn't a religious leader at all or even in training to be one. Sometimes we include her when we talk about Jesus' disciples, but when Matthew, Mark, Luke, and John talk about the Twelve, they don't mean Mary. They mean the men who were personally called to join the movement: Peter, James, John, and the rest. Those men knew that preaching was in their future, and they got a front-row seat in class for three years, and Jesus even had them organized into preaching small groups so they could practice in pairs, on missionary field trips. They were a seminary class of twelve, with the best supervised ministry placement ever. But Mary? She wasn't in that program, not formally, anyway. She was just someone who loved Jesus and wanted to follow him.

She was also someone with a past. Not necessarily a racy one; the prostitute gossip is mostly a Middle Ages invention that Scripture doesn't support. Mary's past was that she used to have seven demons.[1] That's enough disease, mental illness, and chronic pain for an entire neighborhood—and for the record, more than anyone else in Jesus' inner circle ever had to contend with. We can only guess what the demon-tormented Mary used to be like, talking to herself on the bus, or confined to bed for months, or slumped in the corner with a needle in her arm; demons take many forms. Jesus cast out every last one of them, and Mary loved him for it, but he couldn't erase the collective memory of who she used to be. It trailed along behind her like a shadow. It was how people identified her: "This is Mary, the woman who used to have seven demons, until Jesus cast them out, apparently with no side effects, but you never know, so be aware; be careful. . . ." She might as well have had a sign around her neck, like some carnival sideshow, exhibit A for epic exorcism. And it seems like people found it easier to read the sign and leave it at that than to ask her to speak for herself. We don't know how Mary told her own story or if she ever did. We never hear her say, "This is what the realm of God looks like, to me." The disciples got to practice that sort of speech. We don't know if Mary did.

---

1. See Mark 16:9 and Luke 8:1–3.

On Easter morning, all that changed. Not because Mary suddenly got promoted to the upper ranks of discipleship or was voted to fill the newly vacant spot among the Twelve, now that Judas had effectively crashed and burned; she wasn't. Mary never meant to start preaching. She'd gone to the tomb to weep, and that was it. It's what we do when someone we love has died: we just grieve. Sit down next to the body and cry. Hold it one more time, do what we can to prepare it for burial, say good-bye, cry all over again. It doesn't sound like anything a preacher would do to prepare a sermon, but after reading this story, maybe we should think about it. A preacher might start by just crying. Go to the tomb of what the empire has murdered, and lament.

Jesus didn't die of natural causes. His death was plotted. It was staged. It was meant as a warning: *Don't you ever rise up to challenge the power of Rome. We will break you. We will desecrate your body. Your mother will have to watch. And no one with any sense will stand by you.* Crucifixion is an abomination that finds equivalents in every age, and it is designed to intimidate the witness. But grief is a form of resistance, and Mary didn't hide from that grief. She seized it, walked right into it. The other disciples were hunkered down in a locked room, trying to be sensible—strategize about survival and interim leadership and such. Mary didn't follow that logic. She got up early in the morning while it was still dark and went to the tomb, because that's what we do when someone we love, something we believe in, has died. We just grieve.

There's a plot twist, of course. Nobody expects resurrection. The Spanish Inquisition, maybe, but not the resurrection. Mary saw the stone had been rolled away from the tomb and the body moved, and she ran back to tell the disciples, who came to see for themselves (making sure to report who ran the fastest and got there first, because competitive discipleship: *that's* important). Sure enough, the tomb was empty. The disciples took one look and left; this was not a crime scene they wanted to be involved in. But Mary stayed and wept some more. And now there was even more to cry about. Someone had taken away her Lord, and she didn't know where they had laid him. Someone had stolen his body. And really, what other explanation could there be? When the Jesus we know doesn't stay in the place where we've put him (and that happens in more ways than we like to admit), isn't somebody to blame for moving him out of our reach?!

They've taken away my Lord, and I don't know where they've laid him. That's a refrain a person can hear a lot, when seminary students take their first master's-level Bible course: "They've deconstructed my Jesus, and I don't know where they've left him!" But it's a refrain we hear in other places too. Church folk might say it when there's new music in the worship service: "They've replaced my Jesus, and I don't know where they've put him!" Preachers might say it, when they go to the biblical text expecting one thing and find it's pulled the rug out from under them, disrupting whatever they were planning to say in the sermon: "This text has rebooted my Jesus, and I don't know where he is, and I don't have time on a Saturday night to look!" When Jesus doesn't stay in the place where we've put him, it's so easy to point fingers and cast blame. It might even be our first instinct as human beings, because nobody expects resurrection from an empty tomb. And before you know it, our graveyard grief has shifted focus. We aren't crying for a crucified Jesus. We're weeping over a stolen body, and everyone we meet is a potential thief.

This is where Mary finds herself. Jesus appears right in front of her, and she can't even recognize him in the state she's in; she thinks that he's the gardener and that *he* stole the body. "Sir," she begs him, "if you've taken him away, tell me where you've laid him, and I'll deal with it"—which is probably code for "Look, I won't go to the police. Just show me the body, and we'll pretend it never happened." It's how a grief-crazed person reacts to the shock of death and, ironically, how a sensible preacher might try to end the story: if the empty tomb is unsettling, if it upends too much too fast, if it flouts the laws of nature—well, let's smooth it over. Let's rewind and put Jesus back where he was, before all the change and craziness happened.

Two things happen at this juncture. The first is that Jesus calls her by name: "Mary!" When we're crying about who took our Jesus away, that may be the only thing that will stop us. We have to hear him say our name. Maybe we can't see resurrection any other way, and we *have* to see it, because we can't ever *explain* it. If we could explain it, Jesus would have said, "I believe you're operating with a false hermeneutic, Mary. Sit down and let me interpret these events for you." We can't explain resurrection. It addresses us; it calls us out. "Mary!" That's all Jesus has to say, and she knows. There isn't any stolen body. There's a *risen* body! And what are the first words out of her mouth? A confession: *"Rabbouni!"*—which doesn't mean "teacher" at all, but "My Lord. My Lord!"

We can guess what Mary tried to do next. She tried to embrace him: that's the second thing that happens. Jesus says, "Stop holding onto me; stop clinging to me." Call it the first post-resurrection teaching: *Stop holding onto Jesus.* We can see the risen Christ, but we can't cling to him. We can confess our faith in Jesus, but we can't own him. Jesus is loose in the world, and no tomb of expectations is going to hold him down.

It's an amazing moment, this embrace, because it shows us how quickly it can happen, how we are almost programmed as human beings to harden our experience into universals. One moment of absolute clarity sparks an embrace, and we make our confession of faith—and then we can't let it go. We start to cling to it and control it and defend it and measure others against it, until before we know it, we think we can judge what resurrection looks like. "My Lord!" turns into "*My* Lord; *mine!*" Like clockwork: remarkable. And thank God for Mary, who shows us what the sequence looks like, and does it with such grace and purity. Her embrace is an act of love, and Jesus knows it, but he also knows the flip side of that act, what it could become. It's a teachable moment. "Don't hold onto me. Stop clinging to me. But listen, Mary: I have some other verbs to give you. Go and tell."

And she does. She lets go of him, the Jesus she knew and loved, and she goes out—not to write the church's first creed, but to preach the church's first sermon: "I have seen the Lord." No doctrine. No explanation. Just testimony to what she saw and what she believes. And there is no guarantee that out there in the world, people will accept it, no guarantee at all that they will hear her as a credible witness. Given who she is and who she used to be, they probably won't. But Mary is the one who showed up at the tomb, so she's the one who is sent. Now there is only the hope that her life as a disciple will confirm what she says, which is that Christ has died, Christ is risen, and Christ will come again. *Go and tell.*

Is this all it takes to be a preacher? Yes, if this story in John 20 has anything to say about it. But let's be honest: there's a disconcerting quality to it, because what John 20 says about preaching isn't what the church usually says. Who does Jesus commission for the first Easter sermon? A woman with no training, few credentials, and a rather disturbing past. Seven demons. Can we really be sure they haven't scarred her irreparably? Can we trust her with a leadership role? What if she says something inappropriate or doctrinally unsound?! This is not the person you and I might pick to best represent the church and deliver the Easter message. But look here: Jesus does. This is who he picks to preach to the likes of you and me, and before we ever speak any words ourselves, maybe we should listen to Mary's. Apparently, she's met the risen Christ in ways we haven't because we were thinking about our own survival and stayed home. She went looking for Jesus. And she found him, and then found us, to tell us about it.

Maybe preaching, whatever it is, starts with Mary. Maybe she's the one we should be looking for. After all, she was Jesus' first choice to preach the Easter sermon. He always did like a surprise ending.

N

IS FOR

NICODEMUS

John 3

Now there was a Pharisee named Nicodemus, a leader of the
Jews. He came to Jesus by night and said to him, "Rabbi, we
know that you are a teacher who has come from God, for no
one can do these signs that you do unless God is with that
person." Jesus answered him, "Very truly, I tell you, no one
can see the kingdom of God without being born from above."
Nicodemus said to him, "How can anyone be born after having grown old? Can one enter a second time into the mother's
womb and be born?" Jesus answered, "Very truly, I tell you,
no one can enter the kingdom of God without being born of
water and Spirit. What is born of the flesh is flesh, and what is
born of the Spirit is spirit. Do not be astonished that I said to
you, 'You must be born from above.' The wind blows where
it chooses, and you hear the sound of it, but you do not know
where it comes from or where it goes. So it is with everyone
who is born of the Spirit." Nicodemus said to him, "How can
these things be?" Jesus answered him, "Are you the teacher of
Israel, and yet you do not understand these things?"

John 3:1–10

*N*icodemus is best known for his role in the third chapter of John,
when he asks the questions that launch Jesus' famous "born from
above" speech. He shows up again in the seventh chapter, during a
heated debate about what to do with the rabbi from Galilee, and then
again in the nineteenth, when he brings an extravagant amount of
spices to bury Jesus' body. Tradition has been kind to Nicodemus.

He's held up as an example of faith and a model of generosity: the Pharisee who eventually came around.

But to be frank, it took a while. Which is exactly what John wants us to notice in Nicodemus's story: those of us with a lot to lose seem to take longer to come around. It's not that we don't hear Jesus' call to discipleship. We just take our time acting on it, which has cost and consequences for those around us.

Listen, for example, to how John introduces Nicodemus, in the third chapter of his Gospel. "Now there was a Pharisee named Nicodemus, a leader of the Jews. He came to Jesus by night."

In good writing, first impressions matter. And John, who is especially careful about constructing his beginnings ("In the beginning was the Word" is one of the best openings of a book ever), tells us two important things about Nicodemus right off the bat. One is that Nicodemus's day job earns him considerable power and respect. The other is that he comes to Jesus not in the light of day, when everyone can see, but under cover of night. And if it strikes us as odd that a respectable leader with power in the community would wait until dark to visit the Light of the World, then we're tracking right where John wants us to look.

He came to Jesus by night. The words evoke a sense of mystery and secrecy, a netherworld of fog and intrigue, because nighttime visiting is an out-of-the-ordinary enterprise. And "by night" is different from "at night." A person who comes at night just comes late, when the household has gone to bed. A person who comes by night doesn't want to be seen or caught. There might be shady business dealings or covert operations or furtive matters of the heart. Or we might just need to stay off the record here—which was Nicodemus's situation. The man had questions he didn't want to ask in front of his esteemed colleagues, and he didn't want to be seen asking them either. Questions like:

Are you really a teacher who comes from God?
How can a person truly be born from above?
Is it still possible for us if we have grown old?
How can these things be?!

On the face of it, these hardly seem like eye-popping, head-turning, earth-shattering questions, but that may be the language of the third chapter of John: the words "born from above" might not shock us as they did Nicodemus. We've heard them before. We've heard them *a lot* (or at least the "born again" version). The words may mean different things to us, but they're part of the vernacular. And seekers of faith have been wrestling with questions like these for centuries, trying to shed as much light on their mysteries as the heavens might choose to lend.

But for Nicodemus, these were new and explosive lines of thought. He wanted the dialogue but not the risk to his good name and reputation. He came to Jesus by night for a private audience, and he left the same way—which is to say, unchanged. He wasn't ready to stand up and act on Jesus' words. He wasn't ready to trade his life of comfort and privilege for the life of discipleship. Instead, he slipped back into the night and continued to watch Jesus from afar, letting fear, rather than hope, have the upper hand.

The seventh chapter of John picks up where the story left off, and it's more of the same. Nicodemus and his esteemed colleagues are conferring with the local authorities about what to do with Jesus of Nazareth. The discussion gets heated, and a number of regional stereotypes are hurled Jesus' way. Arrest seems imminent, a guilty verdict all but assumed. Nicodemus clears his throat and cautiously raises his hand. "Our law does not judge people without first giving them a hearing to find out what they are doing, does it?" he asks, mildly (7:51). The correct answer, as everyone knows, is "Right! Everyone gets a fair hearing!" But Nicodemus's colleagues aren't in a mood for legalities. They're out for blood. "Surely *you* aren't from Galilee too, are you?" they jeer. "Read the Scriptures. *No* prophet is supposed to come from Galilee!"

And without another word, Nicodemus goes down into silence. He won't stand up to them. He won't use his power for justice. He protects it (and his decidedly *un*-Galilean name) from further harm. The next we hear of him, Jesus is dead, and Nicodemus has come with a hundred pounds of spices to take away the body. That's an extravagant gesture and an expensive burial, to be sure. But it's also too much too late. We're left wondering what might have been, if Nicodemus had acted on his first conversation with Jesus—if he'd not only recognized the light coming into the world but followed it with his whole heart.

Nicodemus turns up in the life of every one of us, at some point. We can spot him at the council meeting when the pressure to vote with an angry majority becomes almost more than we can bear. We can glimpse him when our courage wavers and we decide not to say that thing we were going to say. Every time we hide a piece of ourselves to ask the questions that trouble us, Nicodemus is the one wringing his hands and worrying on our behalf: "Wouldn't it be wiser to wait? Is today really the day to speak up?"

But Nicodemus is also the one who reminds us that change is possible, even for the most venerable teachers of Israel. Coming to Jesus by night isn't the only option. Neither is paying for his funeral.

Maybe this is a story to read over and over, as we age. No matter how wise we are, no matter how many degrees we hold, no matter how respected a member of a faith community we may be or how many years we've spent reading and studying Scripture, there is always more light to see, always. And it may rock our worlds. It may reset our hard drives. One day, we may find ourselves going over an idea or position we thought we'd resolved long ago. And how does a person find energy to begin a new quest, become a new creation after having grown old?!

Nicodemus learned. So can we. When the light of the world is in the world, we must all be born anew.

O

IS FOR

ONESIPHORUS

2 Timothy 1

> May the Lord grant mercy to the household of Onesiphorus, because he often refreshed me and was not ashamed of my chain; when he arrived in Rome, he eagerly searched for me and found me—may the Lord grant that he will find mercy from the Lord on that day! And you know very well how much service he rendered in Ephesus.
>
> 2 Tim. 1:16–18

*T*he epistle writers liked to give shout-outs to friends and acquaintances in their letters. It's one of their most endearing qualities as writers: in between the soaring theological visions and urgent pastoral interventions are lists of names, real people, whom the authors wanted to greet or recognize. Some of those personalized messages are expressions of thanks. Others are commendations or introductions or requests for things to pack: "When you come, bring the cloak that I left with Carpus at Troas, also the books, and above all the parchments" (4:13). Still others are public reprimands, brief yet sizzling reports of who had made the blacklist and why: "Alexander the coppersmith did me great harm; the Lord will pay him back for his deeds" (v. 14). It's a constant reminder that we are reading about real communities of human beings who managed to love, encourage, and annoy one another every bit as much as we do—and who might have thought twice about a few things if they knew their names were going into the best-selling book of all time.

The most moving of these messages are the ones that describe acts of kindness rendered by ordinary people. Paul (or those writing in his name) often mentioned friends who had ministered to him during his travels, and in 2 Timothy we hear a little narrative about a man called Onesiphorus.[1] The name means "one who brings profit," and it's true that for Paul, Onesiphorus did. But that literal translation hardly does justice to what transpired between these two men.

Onesiphorus first knew Paul in Ephesus, but he caught up with him in Rome, where Paul was alone and imprisoned. And there, in repeated visits, Onesiphorus proved himself useful beyond measure. He searched the jails until he found the apostle, chained in his cell. He refreshed Paul's body and spirit with loving presence and (one assumes) a few nourishing meals. And most meaningful to Paul, and poignant for us, he wasn't "ashamed" of the chains Paul wore. Whether Onesiphorus had a lot of experience visiting others in prison or he was just a person who could address such things with openness, it seems he took the whole situation in stride. He wasn't the least bit embarrassed *by* Paul or *for* Paul, and sometimes that is the greatest kindness a person can offer.

Paul would go on to write about his jail cell experience, or at least draw on it for metaphors to make a point. Chains were a key image for him, and *he* wasn't ashamed them either. To the contrary, he saw the ones he'd worn as a useful reminder of his larger purpose.

> Remember Jesus Christ, raised from the dead, a descendant of David—that is my gospel, for which I suffer hardship, even to the point of being chained like a criminal. But the word of God is not chained. Therefore I endure everything for the sake of the elect, so that they may also obtain the salvation that is in Christ Jesus, with eternal glory. (2:8–10)

Would Paul have written words like these before Onesiphorus visited him in Rome? Would he (or those writing in his name) have used the chain metaphor so freely and naturally, and even placed it back-to-back with a description of his own prison time? "I've suffered for

---

1. The name is easier to pronounce than it looks: five syllables, accent on the third syllable, "On-e-SIF-o-rus."

the gospel and been chained like a criminal, but the word of God is *not* chained!" Paul declared—and maybe Onesiphorus was the inspiration for those lines. Small acts of kindness are magnified during a difficult time. We reflect on them later and remember them: the volunteer visitor at the hospital the day we got the diagnosis, who sat with us until family members could get there; the person in the next seat on the flight home for the funeral, who listened to our stories of regret without judgment; the friend who continued to call and check in on us long after everyone else assumed we were over the grief; the neighbor who made sure we got a hot meal and a place at her kitchen table to do homework on the nights our parents had to work late. These are the people we remember—perhaps for years—in prayer, as Paul did. We may use words very similar to his: *God, refresh them, as they refreshed me. Grant mercy to their households, as they granted it to mine.*

For Onesiphorus, it might have been the most natural thing in the world to be unashamed and unembarrassed by Paul's predicament. Maybe he thought it no big deal, no great sacrifice, to visit Paul in prison and bring him a few comforts from home. But for Paul, it was a very big deal indeed, and one he always remembered. Small acts of kindness can refresh a spirit, inspire an apostle, and summon forth the Word of God—unchained.

P

IS FOR

POET

Matthew 15

Jesus left that place and went away to the district of Tyre and
Sidon. Just then a Canaanite woman from that region came out
and started shouting, "Have mercy on me, Lord, Son of David;
my daughter is tormented by a demon." But he did not answer
her at all. And his disciples came and urged him, saying, "Send
her away, for she keeps shouting after us." He answered, "I was
sent only to the lost sheep of the house of Israel." But she came
and knelt before him, saying, "Lord, help me." He answered, "It
is not fair to take the children's food and throw it to the dogs."
She said, "Yes, Lord, yet even the dogs eat the crumbs that fall
from their masters' table." Then Jesus answered her, "Woman,
great is your faith! Let it be done for you as you wish." And
her daughter was healed from that moment.

Matt. 15:21–28

*T*his is a story a teacher might assign to seminary students who are
feeling a little uptight christologically, the ones who are having a
hard time letting Jesus be his very own messiah without their help.
It's a normal stage of development for seminarians: they love Jesus,
love his message, and want to be his personal bodyguard to protect
him from any negative publicity. The main concern appears to be
that if we were ever to question Jesus, take issue with his actions, or
photograph him in a light that is less than perfect, it would damage
our Lord's reputation with the general public, cause him emotional
pain, and jeopardize the entire kingdom of God project. So instead,
we're all supposed to maintain a respectful distance and keep singing

praise songs, which works great until we open our Bibles to Matthew 15: *It's not fair to take the children's food and throw it to the dogs.*

The story about Jesus and the Canaanite woman can be hard on a seminarian. It's hard on the rest of us, for that matter. How do we explain something like this? Jesus, a Jewish boy from Nazareth, does what other Jewish boys at the time do: he calls someone who isn't Jewish a dog. Which is not a compliment, by the way. It's an ethnic slur. It's a word that's meant to put somebody down. And there it is on the lips of the Prince of Peace, who really needs to work on his metaphors.

This is not an easy story to explain. It kind of makes you want to take Jesus into the kitchen and give him a good talking-to, the way his mother might have done if she'd been there with the disciple boys ("This is not a word your mama raised you to use, and you know it!"). But since the damage is done—after all, he said it; they printed it—we don't have much choice but to try and contain it. Spin it right, and maybe we can protect Jesus from his own story, which is what a lot of very well-meaning Bible scholars have done: focused on that one image, "dog," and tried to explain it. Here are a few samples. (These are real.)

Jesus was just joking.
He was just engaging in a little Middle Eastern banter.
He was just testing the woman to see if she really did have faith.
He didn't mean she was literally a dog! Or as ugly as one!
This is just a literary device.
And he was just clarifying his boundaries for her.
He was just reminding her that he was Jewish, and she wasn't.
And the rule was, Jews first, this time around.
There was only one of him.
You couldn't expect him to heal everyone he ever met.
And remember, after all, he was stressed.
He was tired.
He was off duty.
He didn't want anyone to know he was there.
He wasn't in his healing mode.
And *she* was a real pain in the neck.

> She kept badgering him.
> She couldn't take no for an answer.
> You know what that's like, when you're tired, and someone just
>   won't give it a rest!
> You understand, don't you?

Of course, we do. Every one of those explanations is plausible. And if it's really important to protect Jesus from his own story (since a man who uses words like *that* had better have a bodyguard or a big stick when the wrath comes down), it's understandable that a person might pick one. But if it isn't important to protect Jesus—if he truly can save the world all by himself without our help—then maybe there are other ways to read this story and other ways to hear it. Maybe we don't have to be bodyguards. We could try something else.

Poets, for instance. We could try to be poets, or to think and hear the way they do. A poet's medium is language, after all, just like Scripture, and language is powerful. It does things. It creates things. "In the beginning was the Word, and the Word was with God, and the Word was God," John writes; and it was so (John 1:1). Language can wound and it can mend. "Just say the word, Lord, and my servant will be healed," the centurion declared; and it was so (Matt. 8:8). Jesus takes language seriously, and as people of faith, so do we. What happens if we look at this from a poet's perspective?

Mary Oliver, that rock star of a poet, wrote a little book called *A Poetry Handbook,* in which she talks about how poems are built and read and understood. So much of it applies to Scripture that we could think of it as a Scripture handbook too. In the book, Oliver covers all the categories when it comes to poetry: meter and rhyme, form and diction, sound and sense and imagery. And imagery is where Jesus gets into trouble: *It's not fair to take the children's food and throw it to the dogs.*

From a poet's perspective, the problem isn't that the word "dog," that image, is offensive. It's that it's so unoriginal! In Jewish Palestine during this period, you'd hear the word on the street every day. It was the epithet of choice when it came to Canaanites, and everyone used it and believed it too—that *those people* weren't clean, they weren't civilized, they didn't believe in God, and they talked fun-ny.[1] They just weren't very evolved—and how could they be, when they were descendants of Ishmael, Abraham's illegitimate son?! Jews were descendants of Isaac, the son who was promised. And Jesus was sent to the lost sheep of the house of Israel, not to flea-bitten Canaan-ites who wouldn't recognize a word of God if they tripped over it. *It's not fair to take the children's food and throw it to the dogs.*

Mary Oliver would say that this is not poetic language, because the dog metaphor is a cliché. And clichés don't work in poems, she says, or for that matter, in any other type of language either. They don't take us anywhere we haven't already been.

This had to have been the case for the Canaanite woman. How many times in her life had she been called a dog? This could hardly have been the first, which isn't to say that it wouldn't hurt. When someone aims a word at us the way they aim a rock, it hurts, always. But it's nothing new. It doesn't take us anywhere we haven't already been—and poetic language does. Poetic language makes us look twice. It has to stop us in our tracks so we can rethink what is going on. Like this exchange between the woman and Jesus:

> He answered, "It is not fair to take the children's food and throw it to the dogs." She said, "Yes, Lord, yet even the dogs eat the crumbs that fall from their masters' table."

There are so many ways to respond to that word, "dog," in a moment like this. We can endure it in bruised silence or dignity. We can refute it ("No sir, I am not a dog") or return it in kind ("So I'm a dog, am I? Well, you're a big-headed, circumcised son of an Aramean"). We can escalate the verbal violence, insult for insult, until words turn into fists, and fists into guns, and guns into wars that never end; it happens all the time. Or we can find another way, as the Canaanite woman did. We can reach down, pick up that word "dog," and break it open into something new—which is exactly what poets do. They take our tired old language with its unoriginal and hurtful clichés, and they break

---

1. It goes without saying (I hope) that these descriptions and the ones following are meant to be read ironically, if not sardonically. Racial and ethnic slurs are always offensive.

it open so we can see what we have been hiding behind. And they do it without sticks or stones or fists or guns; they do it with words. In the beginning there's always a word. The Canaanite woman knew that. She was quick to send a few words Jesus' way, when called for, spoken as well as unspoken. Like these, perhaps.

> It's not fair to take the children's food and throw it to the
>   dogs?
> Well, maybe you're right.
> Dogs don't get a place at the table, do they?
> They sit in the corner in a down-stay, without begging.
> Because good dogs aren't allowed to beg.
> They have to wait until everyone at the table is finished.
> They have to wait for the word—for the master's word.
> And then they can eat whatever fell on the floor.
> They can eat the crumbs and be satisfied.
> They can eat the crumbs and be grateful.
> They can eat the crumbs and be healed, if it's the right
>   kind of bread!
> So yes, sir, you're right: it's not fair to take children's
>   food and throw it to dogs.
> But even dogs are thankful for the bread crumbs that fall
>   from your table.
> Even dogs can't wait for you to take your bread and
>   bless it—
> And break it so the crumbs fly and fall.
> So go ahead, sir. Have your supper.
> Break your bread. Break it well. I'll wait.

Mary Oliver says a poem is a confession of faith. "It is not an exercise. It is not word play. Whatever skill or beauty it has, it contains something beyond language devices, and it has a purpose other than itself. Yes indeed," she says, "for poems are not words after all, but fires for the cold, ropes let down to the lost, something as necessary as bread in the pockets of the hungry. Yes indeed."[2]

---

2. Mary Oliver, *A Poetry Handbook: A Prose Guide to Understanding and Writing Poetry* (New York: Ecco, 1994), 122.

The Canaanite woman may not have needed to speak like a poet if she hadn't had a daughter who needed the word. And this is what Jesus saw, eventually. "For saying that, you may go," he told her. "The demon has left your daughter." She went home and found it so. And Jesus, when he left the region, must have remembered the day, and thought about it. Every time he took the bread in his hands, he must have thought about the woman who came and knelt before him, with such fire for what he could give. Jesus recognized a good confession when he heard one. He recognized good poetic language too. And he must have torn his bread with a little more abandon after this, so the crumbs would be sure to fly.

The world is waiting for us to be poets—or use words as poets do—and speak our faith against the tired clichés of this world. There are plenty of defeated words out there, plenty of defensive words, plenty of killing words, laced with bombs. But there are other words too. And they make us think twice and turn around, and repent and believe, and begin again.

Maybe this is our work: to offer the bread of life and, as Mary Oliver would say, "the cup of astonishment."[3] Break it one word at a time, just one. Yes indeed.

3. Mary Oliver, "Everything," in *New and Selected Poems,* vol. 2 (Boston: Beacon Press, 2007), 4.

Q

IS FOR

QUIRINIUS

Luke 2

> In those days a decree went out from Caesar Augustus that all
> the world should be registered. This was the first registration
> and was taken while Quirinius was governor of Syria.
>
> Luke 2:1–2

*L*uke tells us that Quirinius was the Roman governor in charge when
Jesus was born. Scholars have pointed out that Luke's dates are a bit
off: historical records place Quirinius in Syria a few years before or
after Jesus' birth, and the census Luke refers to probably happened in
another year too. It's a discrepancy that has created anxiety in some
circles (can a text that is historically inaccurate still be infallible?) and
glee in others (can a text that is historically inaccurate still be taken
seriously?!), and getting sucked into the drama is easier than one
would think. But it also distracts us from the bigger literary objective.
Luke is making a point about what it means for Jesus to be born at a
particular time and place in history, with this set of political realities;
what it looks like when heaven and earth intersect, and God decides
that Judea, under Roman occupation, would be an excellent backdrop
for incarnation.

So here's what it looked like, according to Luke chapters 1 and
2, the year God picked a woman and a man from Nazareth to have a
baby Messiah:

> Quirinius was governor.
> Augustus was emperor.

Herod was king.

There was a new tax code.

In short, life was hell: a perfect storm of misery. With Quirinius and Augustus and Herod and taxation, how could it be anything else? Luke is letting us know that incarnation had a lot to contend with at that political moment. It was a terrible time for a messiah to be born. Which is to say, maybe it was the perfect time.

Political figures, even those from the ancient world, usually have plenty of historical documentation to give us a sense of what sort of leaders they were. What we know about Quirinius, Augustus, and Herod suggests that—for those living in Judea, at least—these three were a particularly brutal combination to have in power at the same time: ambitious, ruthless, brilliant, and (by some accounts) completely amoral. Between them, they led armies and rejected law, dismantled a republic and replaced it with an empire, discarded wives and executed sons, expanded territories and crushed rebellions, collaborated with enemies and betrayed compatriots, built massive temples and forts for their own protection and glory, and, to pay for it all, imposed taxes that were particularly harsh and burdensome for the poor. Not every historian sees it that way; there are obviously many angles from which to view the narratives and construe the legacies of these three men. But the consistencies between them are enough for us to realize what a dangerous time it was in Judea for Jesus and his family (see "K is for King Herod").

Those who first read Luke's Gospel probably didn't need any introductions to Quirinius, Augustus, and Herod, any more than we need introductions to Hitler, Stalin, and Mussolini. Just saying the names would trigger stories that send shivers down the spine. And it would make the point. Incarnation is always perilous. Evil is always a factor. We cannot ignore the particularities of our own political contexts—how Quirinius is among us now, and what that means for the most vulnerable and poor.

Yet Luke's readers would know something else, too, and so should we. Not even Quirinius can halt the purposes of God. The powers and principalities of this earth may be at work, but they will never defeat the Prince of Peace.

When Jesus was born in Bethlehem of Judea, Quirinius was governor of Syria. Luke insists that we know his name and take it seriously; it matters to the story. Just as it matters who is in power today, in our own cities and states and countries and provinces. And which of them might be Quirinius, or one in the making, and on the rise. The real question, when it comes to historical accuracy and textual infallibility, is whether we will take seriously in *our* day the factual evidence right before us, the political texts that are published and plain. Take them seriously, Luke is saying. Don't underestimate the dramas of distraction. Incarnation has a lot to contend with in *our* political moment. It might be the worst time for Immanuel, God-with-us, to arrive—and also the perfect time. Just knowing that there is reason for hope may be encouragement enough for us to saddle up our own donkeys and turn our faces toward Bethlehem, where a star, and Herod's soldiers, will soon appear.

R

IS FOR

RHODA

Acts 12

> Then Peter came to himself and said, "Now I am sure that the
> Lord has sent his angel and rescued me from the hands of Herod
> and from all that the Jewish people were expecting."
>   As soon as he realized this, he went to the house of Mary,
> the mother of John whose other name was Mark, where many
> had gathered and were praying. When he knocked at the outer
> gate, a maid named Rhoda came to answer. On recognizing
> Peter's voice, she was so overjoyed that, instead of opening
> the gate, she ran in and announced that Peter was standing at
> the gate. They said to her, "You are out of your mind!" But she
> insisted that it was so. They said, "It is his angel." Meanwhile
> Peter continued knocking, and when they opened the gate they
> saw him and were amazed.
>
> Acts 12:11–16

*R*hoda was part of the Jerusalem church in its turbulent early years.
She was also part of a prayer vigil the church held one night for
Peter, who had been arrested and was expected to be executed the
next morning on King Herod's orders, barring a miracle or an act of
God—which is exactly what happened. In the middle of the night, an
angel appeared in Peter's maximum-security jail cell and orchestrated
a prison break, despite chains and guards on every side. Peter, who
thought he must be dreaming, woke up to find himself alone on the
streets of the city without a soldier in sight. He quickly sought shelter
at the home of well-to-do friends, the very ones who were holding

the prayer vigil on his behalf. Peter knocked; Rhoda answered. And recognizing who it was—the answer to all their prayers, right there on the doorstep—she ran into the living room and announced who was at the gate: Peter himself! To which they all responded, "You are out of your mind!"[1]

Rhoda brought good news, and they didn't believe her. She declared their prayers had been answered, and they called her delusional. If this story sounds familiar, it's because it is.

Rhoda gets the same kind of reaction to her news as the women who went to the tomb that first Easter morning, saw visions of angels, and ran back to report it to the disciples—only to be told they were full of *lēros*, a word that has been charitably translated as "folly" or "nonsense" or "idle talk," but really means something much ruder, cruder, and unfit for polite company (as in, "You are so full of !@#$").[2] The response Rhoda got was similar. And not from scoffers and skeptics, as we might expect, but from the community of faith itself, which at that very moment had been praying for just such an outcome, Peter's release and return. They couldn't believe Rhoda's report that it had actually come to pass. Or they couldn't believe it coming from her.

If the latter is the case (and it probably is), the story plummets into a sinkhole of unanswered, lingering questions. Rhoda isn't a "maid," as the NRSVue would prefer us to read. Rhoda is a slave, a girl of indeterminate age, and the property of the well-to-do woman in whose house the church is meeting. And while the early church preached a vision of utopian ideals—"All who believed were together and had all things in common; they would sell their possessions and goods and distribute the proceeds to all, as any had need," Acts 2:44–45 tells us—it is also entirely true that the vision

---

1. See Anna Carter Florence, "Preacher as One 'Out of Your Mind,'" in *Slow of Speech and Unclean Lips: Contemporary Images of Preaching Identity,* ed. Robert Stephen Reid (Eugene, OR: Wipf & Stock, 2010), 144–53.

2. See Luke 24:11 ("But these words seemed to them an idle tale, and they did not believe them"). For more on *lēros* (λῆρος), see Anna Carter Florence, *Preaching as Testimony* (Louisville, KY: Westminster John Knox Press, 2007), 117–19.

wasn't lived out in full.[3] Human enslavement was a fact of life in the Roman Empire, the harsh and bitter aftermath of war, poverty, and human trafficking. Wealthy people, Christians included, owned slaves. They saw no conflict between that and the gospel's message of emancipatory freedom. It seems obvious that this would be the case, given what we know of the world, both ancient and modern. Yet it is hardly discussed or acknowledged, even in our own Bible translations; when we read the word "servant," it usually means "slave." And that changes how we hear the stories. That changes how we hear *this* story. Rhoda, like so many other enslaved persons of her time, was a follower of Jesus, a fervent believer of the gospel. When Peter knocked at the door of the home of Mary, and Rhoda—Mary's slave girl—was sent to answer it, how does it sound to us that she announced Peter's freedom and the answer to their prayers while her *own* freedom was undeniably denied? How does it sound to us that the church folk gathered in Mary's home told Rhoda she was out of her mind for announcing freedom?

In one sense, Rhoda is like Rahab (see "R is for Rahab"), in that she, too, is a kind of stock character we meet often in literature: not the householder, but the servant; in this case, an enslaved girl. These characters may seem secondary, but they never are, and they cannot be underestimated. They possess virtues and strengths that show the weakness of the householder. They work the edges of the story with dignity and grit. And in the end, their resourcefulness saves the day—and exposes the cracks in the system. Or they may *not* save the day, if the story allows for more shadow, and they only lift a veil on the tragedies of this world.

---

3. Margaret Aymer and Emerson B. Powery are two scholars who have written on reading the New Testament—and the story of Rhoda in particular—with a focus on human enslavement. See Margaret Aymer, "Outrageous, Audacious, Courageous, Willful: Reading the Enslaved Girl of Acts 12," in *Womanist Interpretations of the Bible: Expanding the Discourse,* ed. Gay L. Byron and Vanessa Lovelace (Atlanta: SBL Press, 2016), 265–89; and Emerson B. Powery, "Reading with the Enslaved: Placing Human Bondage at the Center of the Early Christian Story," in *Bitter the Chastening Rod: Africana Biblical Interpretation after* Stony the Road We Trod *in the Age of BLM, SayHerName, and MeToo,* ed. Mitzi J. Smith, Angela N. Parker, and Ericka S. Dunbar Hill (New York: Lexington Books/Fortress Academic, 2022), 71–90, esp. 74–80.

Rhoda is announcing freedom, the answer to our prayers. The knee-jerk reaction of those around her is to ignore the truth she brings: *She is out of her mind.* If the story sounds familiar, it's because it is. If it appears to invite us to hold open a door that leads to reflection and reckoning, that's because it does. And behind that door is a freedom the church as a *whole* body has yet to live into. But Rhoda stands ready. She is poised to speak.

S

IS FOR

SHIPWRECK

Acts 27

> When it was decided that we were to sail for Italy, they trans-
> ferred Paul and some other prisoners to a centurion of the
> Augustan Cohort, named Julius. . . .
>
> Since much time had been lost and sailing was now danger-
> ous, because even the Fast had already gone by, Paul advised
> them, saying, "Men, I can see that the voyage will be with dan-
> ger and much heavy loss, not only of the cargo and the ship,
> but also of our lives." But the centurion paid more attention to
> the pilot and to the owner of the ship than to what Paul said.
>
> Acts 27:1, 9–11

*T*he Mediterranean Sea is one of the most dangerous places in the
world to sail because of how many islands there are, hundreds of them,
springing up in every direction; some large, like Crete and Cyprus;
some small, like Cabrera and Capri. Some are so small they won't
make it onto a map, but they can mess with a ship—and sink it too. The
islands conceal reefs, and the reefs change currents and shift winds,
until mariners don't know in which direction to go. There are seasons
when it isn't safe to sail at all because the storms are so unpredictable.

That's the issue in our story: Paul's ship has missed the window
of opportunity for safe voyage to Italy. Winter is coming. If they set
out now, they are sure to run into rough weather, and there won't be
a coast guard to come after them. (Read the chapter. It's so filled with
detail, it sounds like a sailor wrote it.) Paul was a prisoner on board
the ship, bound for trial in Rome, with a centurion named Julius who
had been assigned to him. And while Paul wasn't a sailor, he'd been

traveling these waters long enough to know the ship was headed for trouble. The winds were against them, and they'd already lost too much time. "If we continue our journey," Paul warned, "we're in danger of heavy losses—the cargo, the ship, and our lives."

No one paid any attention. The centurion was kind to Paul, but he wasn't about to take a prisoner's advice over that of the ship's owner and the pilot, both of whom thought their best option was to keep sailing. "If we leave now," the pilot and owner assured the centurion and the crew, "we can beat the storms, and winter in the next port. And not lose all the profits either." (Although they probably said that last bit to themselves.)

But they were wrong. A storm did come, a terrible northeaster, as the story puts it, and the ship was caught square in the pounding wind and the waves. For days, the crew battled to stay afloat, even resorting to throwing the cargo and tackle overboard to lighten the ship's load. And after days and days in the storm, as they were giving up hope, Paul stood up. He wasn't the captain or the pilot of that ship, or the owner or a crew member, or a centurion or soldier or a passenger of any rank at all. In fact, Paul the prisoner was the lowest-ranking person among them, not at all the one they would ordinarily look to for leadership at such a time. But he'd been given a message, a word from the Lord, to give them hope. He stood up among them and spoke:

> "Men, you should have listened to me and not have set sail from Crete and thereby avoided this damage and loss. I urge you now to keep up your courage, for there will be no loss of life among you, but only of the ship. For last night there stood by me an angel of the God to whom I belong and whom I worship, and he said, 'Do not be afraid, Paul; you must stand before the emperor, and, indeed, God has granted safety to all those who are sailing with you.' So keep up your courage, men, for I have faith in God that it will be exactly as I have been told. But we will have to run aground on some island." (vv. 21b–26)

Paul's words are a little terrifying, but then, so is the storm, and it won't do any good to make light of it. They can't pretend things aren't what they are. And in a terrifying moment, to hear the terrifying truth can be strangely comforting. "We aren't going to die; no one will die. But we *will* have to wreck the ship. And run aground on some island."

A moment of crisis can snap us into laser focus like nothing else can. What is the real disaster here? What is of utmost importance? What is it we most fear, and what is it we think we can't recover from? Loss of cargo? Loss of ship? Loss of life itself? From the middle of a storm, each is possible, and each will have its share of voices arguing on its behalf.

The ship's owner and the pilot, for instance, have made it perfectly clear that for them loss of cargo is the biggest fear, and delivery of it, with profits, is the primary concern. We know this from their actions a few verses back. They were willing to keep sailing through waters they knew would be perilous, risking the lives of 276 souls aboard—and the wreckage of the ship as well. And all for the chance to complete the journey and cash in on the cargo the ship was carrying. That's a lot to gamble and a terrible price to pay, but people do, all the time, or have others do it with *their* lives. It's the cost of doing business, the ship's owner and the pilot might say. Loss of life, loss of ship: it's a risk we live with and a gamble we take.

The soldiers aboard the ship have another option to argue. For them, loss of *some* lives is the biggest fear. They propose to kill all the prisoners before abandoning ship, so none will have the chance to escape (v. 42). The soldiers can see that loss of ship and loss of cargo are imminent; they're even willing to run aground on some island. But they don't want *their* lives in danger, down the road, if a prisoner who was supposed to be in their charge should make a run for it and turn up a few islands away. With wreckage imminent and the lifeboats cut, loss of life seems inevitable; they can't save everyone. Loss of *my* life is the primary concern. Every man for himself.

In a shipwreck, all is chaos, and panic is only human. So are the frantic voices arguing over risk factors and sustainable losses. But Paul brings the sharp sword of the Word of God to cut through the noise. *The only thing that matters here is life. The only thing worth saving here is life. The cargo can go. The ship can go. Those things don't matter; pick up the pieces and go on. We can survive running aground on some island. Stay together, and we will save all our lives.*

Some of us are watching the church in these days, with its shrinking numbers that we measure so carefully. For many, it feels like a perfect storm, a confluence of every disaster factor that can bring a ship down, all converging on the church at once. We've cut loose all the cargo we think we can afford to lose. We've cut loose the ship's tackle to lighten its load. But shipwreck seems imminent, and the frantic voices are competing for a hearing. Which do we listen to? The ship's owner and pilot, who would sacrifice anything to save the cargo? The soldiers on board, who would sacrifice some lives, but not others? What if we lose both ship *and* cargo? Will we still be the church, without them? Will we be a church at all, if we have to run aground on some island?

People who lived through the Great Depression often told stories about what those awful years were like. One woman described how her family lost everything, practically overnight. They had been quite well-to-do, and then one day, they didn't have a cent to their name. "I used to think I couldn't get along without my things," this woman would tell her great-grandchildren, smiling, "and then I learned that I could." It was an Acts 27 sort of story: there was no loss of life, only the ship and its cargo. They had to run aground on some island. Some family members never recovered from the shock, but this woman did. Shipwreck made her stronger, and her faith stronger as well. Telling the story to her grandchildren and great-grandchildren passed along some of that strength.

After fourteen days in the storm at sea, Paul stood up again to speak to his shipmates. They were starting to turn on each other, as some do in a crisis. Paul knew they couldn't survive if they did, and he knew how hungry they were, because they hadn't eaten for weeks. He took bread and broke it, and gave it to them, urging them to take some food and regain their strength. If they did, he said, he had the same message for them as before: not one of them would lose a hair from their heads if they stayed together and remained a united group. There would be no loss of life in this shipwreck.

Paul's shipmates did as he said, every last one of them. There wasn't a Christian among them, but they ate the bread like the sacrament it was, and their hearts were encouraged, and their hope restored. They ran aground, just as Paul said they would. But they survived it. And the natives on that island of Malta, as Scripture says, showed them unusual kindness.

T

IS FOR

TROAS

Acts 20

> On the first day of the week, when we met to break bread, Paul
> was holding a discussion with them; since he intended to leave
> the next day, he continued speaking until midnight. There were
> many lamps in the room upstairs where we were meeting. A
> young man named Eutychus, who was sitting in the window,
> began to sink off into a deep sleep while Paul talked still lon-
> ger. Overcome by sleep, he fell to the ground three floors below
> and was picked up dead. But Paul went down and bending over
> him took him in his arms and said, "Do not be alarmed, for his
> life is in him." Then Paul went upstairs, and after he had bro-
> ken bread and eaten, he continued to converse with them until
> dawn; then he left. Meanwhile they had taken the boy away
> alive and were not a little comforted.
>
> Acts 20:7–12

*T*roas was a city on the Aegean coast, in Asia Minor, and a place Paul
visited on a few of his missionary journeys. Ships traveling between
Asia and Europe often stopped in Troas; it was a regular port of call
along the Mediterranean trade route, and the busiest and most pros-
perous city of its region. It also had a storied past. The ancient city of
Troy, the setting of Homer's *Iliad,* had once stood on the same peninsula, just a few miles away. The battles of the Trojan War were said
to have been fought nearby. Troas was strategically located for travel
and trade, yes, but also for epic and myth—stories of great heroes and
great conflicts and the gods who took sides. Sailing into the harbor of
Troas, voyagers must have given at least a passing thought to those

tales of old. They may have wondered if the spirits of Achilles and Ajax, Odysseus and Agamemnon, Hector and Priam, Helen and Paris, were still stirring in the waves.

When Paul came to Troas, he had a big story to tell, as epic as any the earth had seen—and in his view, every bit as exciting. It was so epic that it kept him (and the church in Troas) up all night in the telling. And while Paul was surely among the most enthusiastic of bards, he may not have been the most poetic or entertaining. Composing the Christian version of the *Odyssey* doesn't seem to have been his main concern. Paul had things to discuss; he liked to talk. So as the hour grew later, and the lamps burned lower, we read that "Paul talked still longer," which sounds like Scripture's way of telling us that he didn't know when to call it a night. He was leaving the next day, after all. Maybe there were pressing issues or agenda items still to cover. Or maybe he was remembering, from his own classical education, how long it takes to recite the *Iliad* (twenty-five hours) and was just warming up for a sermon marathon.

Listening to Paul on that night in Troas was a packed roomful of believers and interested folk, all crammed into a third-floor room of a house in town. One of those listeners was a young man named Eutychus. He was perched in a windowsill—the only place to sit, or maybe the best place to breathe—and as sermon odysseys that go on past midnight are pretty much guaranteed to lose at least some members of the audience, Eutychus got sleepy. He started to doze off on the window ledge. If he'd been sitting in the middle of the room, someone would have elbowed him to wake him up. But he wasn't; he was sitting on the margins, like a teenager in the balcony, where nobody noticed or thought to look. And this particular balcony, a window ledge on the third floor, was a dangerous place for a boy to sit, let alone drift off: no bars, no railing, and a long way to fall. Epic negligence, we might call it. Or simply what happens when the needs and concerns of vulnerable groups are pushed to the side. People fall through the cracks and over the ledge. Even at church.

The next we hear, Eutychus has fallen asleep and tumbled out the window—not into the bushes, which would make this a funny story, but onto the hard ground, which makes it a tragic story. He's picked up dead, every bit as dead as Hector's son, Astyanax, who was thrown from the city walls of Troy. The talking stops, the adults are stricken, and as they rush downstairs to the boy's side, Paul takes Eutychus into his arms and says an odd thing: "Do not be alarmed, *for his life is in him.*" The boy revives, some church members take him away in stunned relief, and Paul goes back upstairs to break bread and continue the discussion until dawn.

Is this a resurrection story? Maybe. On the one hand, it's the church's first record of a young person literally bored to death by preaching: a homiletical low point, though popular with youth groups. On the other hand, Paul's words in raising Eutychus take the story in new and old directions. Luke, the writer of Acts, tells us that Paul "took the boy in his arms," and it's the same phrase he uses in another story with another character, the father of the returning prodigal son.[1] In that parable, the father of the prodigal sees his son from a distance, runs to him and puts his arms around him, because the boy "was dead and has come to life" (Luke 15:32). Luke seems to be asking us to read these stories side by side, thinking about all the ways that children can be lost to us, in all manner of epic myth and foolishness. Out the door when the parents indulge. Out the window when the church ignores. Over the ledge when the culture provides no protection. Down to the hard, cold pavement when the system is set up to marginalize whole sectors of children, with few safety nets to catch them.

But Luke also seems to be asking us to linger over Paul's words, spoken as he bent over Eutychus: "Do not be alarmed, for his life is in him." Not life: *his* life. The boy's life. Still present, still moving, still very much his own. As if Paul had not so much revived it but affirmed it. As if the resuscitation were a communal one, restoring them all to mutual attentiveness and care in the family of faith: "It was a near miss, we almost lost him, but thank God, his life is in him."

We sometimes despair of the widespread absence of youth in our faith communities. We may even complain bitterly about it, citing cultural trends (overly scheduled kids, exhausted parents, sports events on Sundays, school and work demands) and rising secularism. Some think the solution is to hire a riveting youth director, someone

---

1. The Greek word is *epepesen*; it appears in both Luke 15:20 and Acts 20:10

who can hold the young people's attention as well as any digital device and regale them with stories as exciting as Marvel Comics, or even Homer. And there may be wisdom and value in this. We can't reach those we don't prioritize. We can't expect the youth to find Paul's sermon marathons as thrilling as the adults (or maybe just Paul) find them.

But Paul in Troas may be showing us something else, a lesson that even he had to learn. Enthusiasm for our subject matter is well and good, but not if it supersedes all else—like an awareness of our listeners and if they're still awake, and more to the point, where they're sitting. A preacher who goes on and on (and who hasn't heard that?) is a preacher who has stopped paying attention to where the people are. And that poses a danger to an entire community, when we fail to notice the ones in the windowsill, poised to fall. The ones on the edges, pushed to the margins.

And what if we did notice? What if we had such reverence for all listeners and "the life that is in them" that we could spot a danger like that before it happened—before any of our people, especially the young, drifted to the edge of a threatening precipice? If we brought the teenagers down from the balcony, for example, and gave them our full attention. If we paid attention to who might be slumped with weariness and offered good news they could receive with joy.

In the battle of Troy, the gods came down and took sides in the conflict. On a night in Troas, the God of resurrecting power did the same thing and reminded a man that our words are never the subject. Jesus Christ is the subject: the odyssey of God made human, crucified, and risen from the pavement for life abundant. For all of us.

U

UTTERANCE

Acts 2

And when the day of Pentecost was fully come, they were all with one accord in one place. And suddenly there came a sound from heaven as of a rushing mighty wind, and it filled all the house where they were sitting. And there appeared unto them cloven tongues like as of fire, and it sat upon each of them. And they were all filled with the Holy Ghost, and began to speak with other tongues, as the Spirit gave them utterance.

And there were dwelling at Jerusalem Jews, devout men, out of every nation under heaven. Now when this was noised abroad, the multitude came together, and were confounded, because that every man heard them speak in his own language.

And they were all amazed and marvelled, saying one to another, Behold, are not all these which speak Galilaeans? And how hear we every man in our own tongue, wherein we were born? Parthians, and Medes, and Elamites, and the dwellers in Mesopotamia, and in Judaea, and Cappadocia, in Pontus, and Asia, Phrygia, and Pamphylia, in Egypt, and in the parts of Libya about Cyrene, and strangers of Rome, Jews and proselytes, Cretes and Arabians, we do hear them speak in our tongues the wonderful works of God. And they were all amazed, and were in doubt, saying one to another, What meaneth this? Others mocking said, These men are full of new wine.

Acts 2:1–13 KJV

*P*entecost is the day when the church celebrates the gift of the Holy Spirit. It's the official end of the Easter season, fifty days after Easter Sunday, and a very big holiday in the church's calendar—but after church, not so much. Pentecost hasn't really caught on in the wider culture. It's not traditional family time, as in, "So where are you celebrating Pentecost this year?" We don't gather in homes for big meals. We don't exchange presents or throw office parties. We don't set off fireworks, which would be festive and fitting. And what to cook? Some may have inherited a few treasured family recipes for Red Pentecost Cupcakes or Tongues of Flames Barbecue Sauce or even Mighty Wind Baked Beans, but if not, the magazines in the grocery store aren't exactly brimming with ideas. And all this reticence seems a bit lopsided. Pentecost is a birthday party. We might think the church would go all out, as we do for Jesus in December, but we don't, not really. Pentecost is a more understated holiday, modest, as if the church were shy about throwing itself a party or preferred that we *not* make a big fuss, please, about the fact that it's a year older.

Of course, the original Pentecost wasn't understated at all. It was a great big noisy fuss, and a glorious one at that—with wind and fire and, strangest of all, Galileans filled with the Holy Ghost and speaking in other tongues, as the Spirit gave them utterance. (*Utterance.* That's a King James word, and a very elegant one.) No one had been expecting that kind of speech from that particular source. Even the Galileans, who were really just Jesus' Galilee-born-and-bred disciples, were surprised. It interrupted what everyone thought God-talk was supposed to be and who was allowed to do it. And to this day, *utterance* has never been quite the same.

The story opens with the disciples in Jerusalem, waiting around for something Jesus had promised to send them: the Holy Spirit. They'd been waiting a long time, nearly fifty days, because Jesus hadn't said when it would be arriving or even what it was, precisely. The only thing he'd told them is that when this Spirit came upon them, they would receive power to be his witnesses to the ends of the earth. *That* was exciting to contemplate. Something was about to begin, all right; the disciples could feel it. Something was about to be born. But they had no due date for it, and since everybody knows a due date is just an educated guess that a baby mostly ignores, it might not have mattered anyway. The Spirit would come when it was good and ready to come, and nothing they did would hurry this process along. So there they were—all together in one place, as they'd been instructed—looking more and more like nervous parents waiting on a new arrival, rather than fully equipped disciples on the eve of their big mission.

On the fiftieth day, when the Spirit finally showed up, it was right in the middle of another party. The day was Pentecost, which for Jews is already a holiday: the Festival of Weeks, Shavuot, the Jewish celebration of the first fruits of summer and the giving of the law to Moses at Mount Sinai, which takes place fifty days after Passover. Outside in the city streets, the party was under way. Pilgrims from everywhere, "devout Jews from every people under heaven," as the story has it, were pouring into Jerusalem to celebrate. They weren't there just for the Mardi Gras beads. These were faithful Jews from other cosmopolitan places who had come to the city to worship. The disciples from Galilee were right there with them, saying the prayers from their upper-room quarters and multitasking: keeping the feast *and* keeping an eye out, should the Spirit interrupt. And interrupt it did, with its signature flair, just as the celebrations were getting going.

A violent wind rushed through the house, flames shot through the air, and fiery tongues flew down on each of them, setting their own tongues on fire. The most astonishing uproar filled the room as everyone began to talk at once. The disciples were speaking languages they wouldn't have recognized two minutes before. Fluently, flawlessly, as the Spirit gave them utterance. With Galilean accents, since the Spirit seemed to like those too. Coptic, Parthian, Phrygian, Latin, and how many more languages?! The disciples couldn't begin to count. So they kept up the utterance, speaking in all those tongues. It was a great big noisy fuss, and a glorious one at that.

Outside, the Pentecost worshipers heard what was happening. They saw it as the disciples spilled into the street, still uttering away in their myriad languages. And for these cosmopolitan visitors to Jerusalem, none of this made sense. Nothing here was adding up. The disciples looked like country folk, in their so-last-decade clothes, and their accents confirmed it: Galileans! Hicks! Yet here they were, speaking perfect Coptic and Latin and Parthian; and how was this possible, to be able to understand such a person?! How was this possible, that a Galilean knew Phrygian?!—*and* could talk about God with such eloquence and passion! The devout Pentecost worshipers in the capital city, Jerusalem, were amazed and stunned at what they were hearing from the mouths of Galileans. And then reason and sophistication got the better of them, and they started to sneer.

"That gibberish doesn't mean anything! It isn't God-talk! They're filled with new wine!" were the first insults to be lobbed. But other insults followed and continue to this day:

> "That's not anyone we need to listen to! It's a person with no education!"
> "That's not a preacher! It's a layperson who was never ordained!"
> "That's not serious theology! It's a Black woman writing nonsense!"
> "That's not bona fide research! It's lightweight feminist drivel!"
> "That's not a justice movement! It's a parade and an excuse to wear sequins!"
> "That's not a real issue! It's angry people who think they deserve special treatment!"

Aren't those speaking Galileans? How could they be uttering anything that matters to us? For the Pentecost worshipers and visitors to Jerusalem, "Galilean" was shorthand for uncouth, backwoods, and provincial. Galilee was rural Palestine, not urbane and cultured city life. But if we're truthful, the "Galilean" shorthand is one we all use—each of us, in our own contexts—and it's always a reason not to listen. "Aren't those people Southerners? Yankees? Midwesterners? Californians? Mississippians? Texans? Rednecks? City folk? Foreigners? Immigrants? Racist? Queer? Partisan? Religious? Elites?" We all have our Galileans, and *we* are Galileans to someone else. Who knows what the mischievous Spirit might be up to with that?

When the Spirit finally arrived, as Jesus promised it would, it came with some gifts—unexpected ones! As we've learned, the Spirit doesn't just *interrupt*. It interrupts *what we know*. Even devout persons (maybe especially devout persons) will hear a new utterance, as the Spirit gives it. They may be the ones uttering it, too, if the wind blows that way: God-talk in Galilean-speak. Say *that* three times fast. And Peter did, or the equivalent, the day the Spirit arrived;

his utterances were what eventually brought the Pentecost worshipers around. They were "pricked in the heart" by his words, the story goes. He told them about Jesus—another Galilean—and that they could receive the Holy Spirit themselves. "For the promise is unto you, and to your children," he said, "and to all that are afar off, even as many as the Lord our God shall call" (v. 39 KJV).

Three thousand souls were baptized that day. It was the church's official birthday, and they went all out, because that's what they'd come to Jerusalem to do: to gather for a holiday. To set off fireworks. To celebrate Pentecost and the first fruits of summer.

V

IS FOR

VOICE

John 10

"The one who enters by the gate is the shepherd of the sheep. The gatekeeper opens the gate for him, and the sheep hear his voice. He calls his own sheep by name and leads them out. When he has brought out all his own, he goes ahead of them, and the sheep follow him because they know his voice. They will not follow a stranger, but they will run from him because they do not know the voice of strangers." Jesus used this figure of speech with them, but they did not understand what he was saying to them.

So again Jesus said to them, "Very truly, I tell you, I am the gate for the sheep. All who came before me are thieves and bandits; but the sheep did not listen to them. I am the gate. Whoever enters by me will be saved and will come in and go out and find pasture. The thief comes only to steal and kill and destroy. I came that they may have life and have it abundantly."

John 10:2–10

I am the gate. Some metaphors in Scripture should probably come with a user's manual, or at least an admission akin to the one John offers here in verse 6: "Jesus used this figure of speech with his disciples, but they had absolutely no idea what he was talking about"—the subtext of which is probably "and chances are you won't understand it the first time around either, so this might not be the best verse to plaster all over highway billboards." To the average reader, *I am the gate* sounds like a gateway slogan to exclusivist thinking. Add the next bit, *whoever enters by me will be saved,* and the church might as well be a club, and Jesus, the bouncer at the door.

And let's be candid. To many, this is exactly what the verse means, and this is exactly who Jesus is: the one and only gatekeeper to God. And since gates require certain tickets or passports for entry, the church (it follows) is the place to get those documents. The church supplies us with the right papers, visas, or answers to present at the border so we can cross over to the other side, where the quality of life (it's said) is undeniably better. Eternal citizenship, as opposed to undocumented existence. Saved, as opposed to not saved. *In,* instead of *out.* We might as well be honest about this: the more politically aligned the church grows, the more it is identified with exclusionary politics and extremist causes. To our increasingly secular world, Christianity's message sounds like one of division, a world carved up into *us* and *them*—with Jesus looking more and more like the armed border patrol.

But let's be clear about this too. Division and exclusion are not the intent of this verse from John's Gospel, and if that's what we hear, it isn't Jesus' voice. The overwhelming message of John's Gospel is in the words Jesus speaks in this very chapter: *I came that they may have life and have it abundantly!* For John, Jesus is the bread of life and the light of the world. The good shepherd and the true vine. The way, the truth, the resurrection, and the life. Jesus' commandment is simple: *Love one another.* And every word he says—*I am the gate* included—must be heard in that key, the key of abundant life.

With that tone in mind, this Scripture sounds very different. Jesus, as John tells us, isn't the gatekeeper. He's simply the gate, which is not a barrier and never was. Its purpose is to mark a boundary of care, the region of pastureland where Jesus' voice can be heard. And we, the sheep, are to listen for his voice so we may have life and have it abundantly.

Sheep are grazing creatures. They require a certain amount of going out and coming in, sunup to sundown, from sheepfold to pasture and back again. If they have a shepherd to guide them, so much the better: the shepherd will call them when it's time to move to greener pastures and will set up the sheepfold where it needs to be. The sheep learn the shepherd's voice and can distinguish it from others. When they hear it, they listen, and when they listen, they are safe: *saved* (if one wants to put it that way), with the pasture and shelter they need, each day. But only if they listen *every* day for the voice that calls to them *throughout* the day. Going out and coming in by the sheepfold gate are daily rhythms of abundant life. The saving lies in hearing which to do, as the shepherd leads.

I am the gate. Metaphors are always occasions to rethink and shake loose our first impressions. Perhaps we're so used to thinking of gates as barricades and walls to keep others out that we can hardly imagine them as thresholds of welcome—and if most of what shapes us is rhetoric of division, it's no wonder. But a gate can be a bridge as well as a barrier. It can lead across and through, back and forth. It can swing open and wide, with free entry and exchange, which in turn fosters rhetoric of connection: *love one another.*

What a world it would be if that message got out—if our lives, not our billboards, were declarations of love. If the voice, not the gate, was what drew our attention. If we listened for the shepherd calling us into life. *By this everyone will know that you are my disciples, if you love one another.*

W

IS FOR

WALKING ON WATER

Matthew 14

> Immediately [Jesus] made the disciples get into a boat and go
> on ahead to the other side, while he dismissed the crowds. And
> after he had dismissed the crowds, he went up the mountain by
> himself to pray. When evening came, he was there alone, but
> by this time the boat, battered by the waves, was far from the
> land, for the wind was against them. And early in the morning
> he came walking toward them on the sea. But when the disci-
> ples saw him walking on the sea, they were terrified, saying, "It
> is a ghost!" And they cried out in fear. But immediately Jesus
> spoke to them and said, "Take heart, it is I; do not be afraid."
> Peter answered him, "Lord, if it is you, command me to
> come to you on the water." He said, "Come." So Peter got out
> of the boat, started walking on the water, and came toward
> Jesus. But when he noticed the strong wind, he became
> frightened, and, beginning to sink, he cried out, "Lord, save
> me!" Jesus immediately reached out his hand and caught him,
> saying to him, "You of little faith, why did you doubt?" When
> they got into the boat, the wind ceased. And those in the boat
> worshiped him, saying, "Truly you are the Son of God."
>
> Matt. 14:22–33

*T*his story in Matthew's Gospel is one that Mark and John tell too,
but slightly differently.[1] In Mark's and John's versions, Jesus is the
only one who walks on water. In Matthew's account, Peter gets to give
it a try too. Peter, the rock of the church—who, true to form, sinks.

---

1. See Mark 6:45–52 and John 6:16–21.

It's the middle of the night and the disciples are at sea, far from shore, the wind against them. Jesus had sent them on ahead to cross to the other side, but they hadn't made much headway. They were lost, scared, and starting to see things, which can happen at 3:00 a.m.—so when they spot a figure walking toward them on the water, they're already so frightened that they think it's a ghost. But it's not; it's Jesus. Of course it is. He comforts them and climbs into the boat, and eventually they make it to shore. Mark and John end the story there. Matthew, however, inserts this odd little exchange between Peter and Jesus, back on the water. As the disciples are recovering from their nearly scared-to-death experience, and before Jesus has a chance to set foot in the boat, Peter jumps up and says, "Lord, if it is you, ask me to come to you on the water."

It's a startling comment, the kind Peter seems to specialize in: abrupt, off topic, and out of the blue. Why would anyone say that?! More to the point, why would anyone want to get out of a boat in the middle of a storm? Wouldn't the logical thing, given the circumstances (dark and stormy night, boat swamped at sea, panicking disciples, a ghost that turns out to be Jesus), be to yell, "Lord, save us!"—and pray that he will? Who would choose to test Jesus in the middle of a crisis, with such a bizarre set of terms?

Peter's words are similar to others we will hear many times in Scripture.

> "If you are the Son of God, turn this stone into a loaf of bread."[2]
> "If you are the Son of God, throw yourself down from here."[3]
> "If you are the Messiah, show us a sign."[4]
> "If you are the Messiah, let yourself down from the cross. Save yourself and us!"[5]

2. See Matt. 4:3 and Luke 4:3.
3. See Matt. 4:6 and Luke 4:9.
4. See John 6:30.
5. See Matt. 27:39–43; Mark 15:29–32; and Luke 23:39.

Jesus is repeatedly asked to prove that he is who he says he is by performing some miracle to someone else's specification—a bait he never takes.

Peter flips the terms around. He doesn't want Jesus to prove his identity by performing a miracle. He wants Jesus to prove his identity by letting *Peter* do the miracle: "Lord, if it is you, ask me to come to you on the water!" The proof of who Jesus is now rests in whether *Peter* can walk on water, which has got to be one of the weirdest conditions a disciple ever set.

Jesus goes with it. "Come on, then," he says, and Peter clambers out of the boat. For a few steps, he does it: he walks on water. He has his proof, if that's what he was asking for, that it really is Jesus. But then he looks down and sees the wind-driven waves, and overcome with fear, he starts to sink. *Now* he says something logical: "Lord, save me!" Jesus immediately reaches out his hand and catches him, saying, "O you of little faith! Why did you doubt?" And the two of them get into the boat.

Peter has had his turn, and now Jesus gets his: *Why did you doubt?* It's a deceptively loaded question, much more loaded than we think. And it instantly begs another: What exactly did Peter doubt? Did he doubt that *he* could walk on water? Or did he doubt that the blurry figure approaching him was really Jesus?

What did Peter doubt? How we answer that question makes a huge difference. Most of the time, to the detriment of all concerned, we seem to pick the first option: *Peter doubted that he could walk on water.*

Answer the question this way, as many of us do, and we can take Peter to task for his lack of faith. His great sin (it follows) is that he didn't keep his eyes on Jesus. He let the wind distract him, and he remembered that fear was a reasonable response. He was afraid, and so he sank. Ah, but if Peter had just had faith, he could have done anything! If he had had faith as a grain of mustard seed, he could have said to Stone Mountain, "Get thee up to Kennesaw," and it would have moved. He could have walked on water for the rest of his life. He could have raised the dead. So the moral of the story (to continue in this line) is "Ya gotta believe!" Have faith in what you can do through the power of Jesus.

It's such a temptation to read the story this way. After all, it would explain a lot, wouldn't it? Whatever is wrong is due to a lack of faith: we didn't have enough of it. We doubted what *we* could do. If we didn't, we could walk on water.

But what if we take the second option? *What did Peter doubt? He doubted that it was really Jesus right in front of him.* "Lord, if it is you," Peter said, "ask me to come to you on the water. Send me." And Jesus did, and it was going fine for a moment, until Peter looked around and remembered that usually people sink in water. With enough wind and waves, boats sink too. And what if this blurry figure *isn't* Jesus, holding out a hand? What if he couldn't tell the difference between Jesus and a ghost? What if he'd only imagined that Jesus would come to them in their distress?

It's a such a temptation to make this story about what *we* can do. But it's not. It's about who *Jesus* is. And here is what Matthew tells us:

> Jesus is the one who will walk on water to be with us.
> Jesus is the one who calls to us over the tumult of the waves.
> Jesus is the one who reaches out a hand to pull us into the boat.

Jesus is the one who sits beside us through and past the storm. We aren't mistaken in that—in his love for us, his care for us, his call to us from wherever we're sinking into a lifeboat of safe passage, and the assurance of his voice above the wind and the waves.

Believe it. And go out to meet him.

IS *IN*

OXEN

Luke 14

One of the dinner guests, on hearing this, said to him, "Blessed is anyone who will eat bread in the kingdom of God!" Then Jesus said to him, "Someone gave a great dinner and invited many. At the time for the dinner he sent his slave to say to those who had been invited, 'Come, for everything is ready now.' But they all alike began to make excuses. The first said to him, 'I have bought a piece of land, and I must go out and see it; please accept my regrets.' Another said, 'I have bought five yoke of oxen, and I am going to try them out; please accept my regrets.' Another said, 'I have just been married, and therefore I cannot come.' So the slave returned and reported this to his master. Then the owner of the house became angry and said to his slave, 'Go out at once into the streets and lanes of the town and bring in the poor, the crippled, the blind, and the lame.' And the slave said, 'Sir, what you ordered has been done, and there is still room.' Then the master said to the slave, 'Go out into the roads and lanes, and compel people to come in, so that my house may be filled. For I tell you, none of those who were invited will taste my dinner.'"

Luke 14:15–24

*G*raduation speeches often feature a version of a saying (variously attributed) that goes like this: "The world is shaped by those who show up." It's a way of advising graduates that gifts, talents, and interests will carry them only so far on the road to glory. In the end, the ones who succeed are the ones who show up—at the drawing board, the keyboard, and the hashing-things-out table—and who keep showing up every day, no matter how badly things went the day before. Commitment. Elbow grease. A very thick skin and a very firm schedule. These are more important than brilliance.

This parable could be Jesus' version of that graduation speech, realm-of-God-style: "The ones who eat bread in the realm of God are the ones who show up at the party." It's Jesus' way of advising his audience that good theology, behavior, and intentions will carry them only so far on the road to salvation. In the end, the ones who feast are the ones who come to the table, no matter how many excellent reasons they have for declining the invitation.

And so many excellent reasons exist! A new piece of land, for instance. Five yoke of oxen, or the new job equivalent. A new marriage partner or other addition to the household. Each has legitimate claims to our time and attention and might be worth excusing ourselves, just this once, right? Reasonable persons understand this. Responsible persons put responsibilities before a banquet—unless the one throwing the banquet happens to be the One Who Created All Things, in which case "reasonable" and "responsible" are in for a little deconstruction.

The parable certainly reminds us that time is of the essence. God's invitation is a summons we can't refuse. And since the invitation is to a banquet, why would we want to turn it down in the first place—a chance to feast in the realm of God? Besides, the clear implication is that if we don't jump at the chance, our places will be filled by others who are worthier, hungrier, and more amenable to persuasion. That house owner is quite determined. He'll compel people to come in from the byways and highways, and they may not look like anyone we'd invite, were it up to us, which will be instructive all around. Better to leave our land, oxen, and honeymoon, and come the first time we're called. Send the RSVP ASAP, make it a yes, and show up.

The message is critical and more necessary by the year, as our life and times get busier. We could customize it to speak even more pointedly into our own particular contexts ("Come to the Communion table to have bread for the journey!" "Slip away to a quiet place for just a few moments, to be still and breathe and pray!" "Show up at

that scriptural banquet table to feast on the Word!"), because everyone can use a reminder to redistribute the priorities when excuses
mount up. God's invitation is a summons, not a suggestion; a drop-
everything-and-come-now affair, not an open house. *Leave the oxen,
take the cannoli*—as soon as God offers them. It's a big spread, this
feast. We won't want to miss it.

Y

IS FOR

YEAST

Luke 13

[Jesus] said therefore, "What is the kingdom of God like? And
to what should I compare it? It is like a mustard seed that someone took and sowed in the garden; it grew and became a tree,
and the birds of the air made nests in its branches."

And again he said, "To what should I compare the kingdom
of God? It is like yeast that a woman took and mixed in with
three measures of flour until all of it was leavened."

Luke 13:18–21

*J*esus had a poet's gift for imagery. He never looked far from home
for it either; the parables he told are filled with everyday things. Seeds
and birds. Brooms and coins. Lamps and baskets. Fathers and sons.
For him, the ordinary world was shimmering with light, and he made
his listeners see it too. He sent them home with new senses. Every
time they picked up a broom, they would remember: "This is what it
looks like when God seeks out the lost. God sweeps the whole house
from top to bottom, searching for us in every corner."

Jesus also had a gift for throwing curveballs. His images of the
ordinary do unusual things in the parables he told; they don't move
in straight lines or yield meaning easily. Take bread, for example,
one of Jesus' most enduring (and for us, sacramental) images. In the
parable of the Yeast, Jesus leaves the dinner table and takes us back
into the kitchen where the bread is made. And what draws his attention is not the finished loaf, freshly baked. It's the dough, in its rising,
or more specifically, what leavens the dough. "What is the realm
of God like?" he asks. "It's like yeast mixed in flour, on its way to

being bread." Which sounds ordinary enough, unless you've tried it yourself and realized how many variables there are.

Bread may be the staff of life with the simplest of ingredients (yeast, flour, water, salt), but the process of making it is not a sure thing. Yeast, the star of the show, is really more of a diva. It's fussy about water temperature. It's exacting about measurements. It requires its allotment of sugars. And sometimes, no matter what you do, it just will not cooperate—behave as it ought or rise as it should—because the house is too chilly, or the dough too wet, or the water too hot, or the moon too full, for all we know. Yeast takes its own sweet time. Like a parable, it will not be hurried, and nothing a person can do will speed the rising. And these are good lessons to learn. Living things have their own sense of timing, and yeast, once it permeates the dough, is a living thing.

"The kingdom of God," says Jesus, "is like yeast that a woman took and mixed in with three measures of flour until all of it was leavened." Perhaps what we could take from this is a message about timing. God's sense of timing is so radically different from our own. What we want to hurry up and plan for and accomplish quickly, God takes seasons of life to bring about; the work is slow and steady and unpredictable. And that's good news for those of us who wonder if God may be doing anything at all these days—in the world, in the church, or in the work we do. We may not see it happening, but it's happening. Trust in God's timing and the slow rise.

Or perhaps this parable has a message for us about ratios. God needs so little to do so much. What we think is minuscule, God can mix into a mountain of flour—and it will be enough to leaven the whole. And that's good news for those of us who see ourselves on the small end of the equation, with shrinking budgets and flagging memberships and only a tiny remnant showing up to do the work. We may not believe it's enough, but it's enough. Trust in God's ratios and the slow rise.

Or perhaps this parable has a message for us about doing a little research when we read Scripture and not trusting everything to translators. The New Revised Standard Version of the Bible states that the woman took yeast and "mixed" it—but that's not quite right. The Greek word is *enkrypto*, which means exactly what it sounds like: encrypted. Concealed. Converted into code that no one else can understand or crack. And if we want the full impact of this parable, we need to reinstate a verb that somehow (oh, the irony) got buried in translation.

It's always nice when the King James Bible sorts things out for us. The translators of that monumental 1611 project got it right the first time:

> And again he said, Whereunto shall I liken the kingdom of God? It is like leaven, which a woman took and hid in three measures of meal, till the whole was leavened. (vv. 20–21 KJV)

The parable takes a tantalizing and unexpected swerve with this change. A *hidden* kingdom of God? An *encrypted* kingdom of God?[1] We could get anxious at this (will we need user names and passwords?!), or we could see the hiddenness as a beautiful mystery, an invitation to a holy quest. Perhaps whatever God is doing isn't deliberately hidden but simply ours to discover. Perhaps a yeast we don't even recognize is at work right now.

The place to start searching could be in the weighty mysteries of the learned. But it could also be in the early mysteries of childhood, a time when the simplest things held wonder and we witnessed them every day. Back in the kitchen where the bread is made, for example, and a small boy stands at his mother's elbow, watching her hands slip yeast into flour and knead the dough and shape the loaf. They won't eat the loaf until it bakes. They can't bake the loaf until it rises. But it will rise, the small boy knows; the miracle happens every day, with a timing only his mother can decipher. And the moment when she hands him the finished loaf to bring to the table where the family is gathered is his first clear memory of heaven.

The realm of God is like yeast that a woman took and hid, and what the yeast looks like, no one knows. We just know it is there—*here*—and will leaven everything in its reach. Even us; all of us. There will be bread enough for the world, and baskets full of leftovers besides.

---

1. My colleague at Columbia Theological Seminary, Jacob D. Myers, teaches a lesson on focus and function to our preaching students in which he invites them to imagine what a difference this translation ("hidden," "encrypted," even "smuggled"!) might make for sermon direction. It's a lively and illuminating session.

Z

IS FOR

ZACCHAEUS

Luke 19

[Jesus] entered Jericho and was passing through it. A man was there named Zacchaeus; he was a chief tax collector and was rich. He was trying to see who Jesus was, but on account of the crowd he could not, because he was short in stature. So he ran ahead and climbed a sycamore tree to see him, because he was going to pass that way. When Jesus came to the place, he looked up and said to him, "Zacchaeus, hurry and come down, for I must stay at your house today." So he hurried down and was happy to welcome him. All who saw it began to grumble and said, "He has gone to be the guest of one who is a sinner." Zacchaeus stood there and said to the Lord, "Look, half of my possessions, Lord, I will give to the poor, and if I have defrauded anyone of anything, I will pay back four times as much." Then Jesus said to him, "Today salvation has come to this house, because he, too, is a son of Abraham. For the Son of Man came to seek out and to save the lost."

Luke 19:1–10

*T*his story doesn't tell us if Zacchaeus was a regular tree climber or especially good at it, agile and nimble, and all geared up with his own spurs and lanyards. It just says Jesus was coming, the streets were mobbed, Zacchaeus was short and didn't want to miss out, so he climbed a tree—maybe for the first time since he was twelve.

How well or how gracefully he climbed doesn't seem to be the point. How *short* he was doesn't even seem to be the point; when the tall guys are in front, everyone behind them and trying to see over them is short. Height is relative. Also metaphorical. For Zacchaeus, this tree-climbing venture was a problem-solving maneuver. It was improv, pure and simple: *Yes, and.* Jesus was passing through Jericho on his way to Jerusalem, and Zacchaeus had to see him, he had to, even if the crowd wouldn't let him through. So he ran ahead, found a sycamore tree along the parade route, climbed up into it (which takes some doing), and, from his leafy perch, waited for Jesus to pass by. It wasn't the most dignified of solutions, but it worked. Now he had a view. An awkward one, but he did.

He might have hoped no one would notice him up there, all out of breath and sweaty faced, with his knees hanging out and his arms scratched up and his clothes askew and awry. The view from the ground of a grown man in a tree, straddling a limb and holding on for all he's worth, isn't the most flattering of angles. It's comical at best and humiliating at worst, and a person could be forgiven for wishing to remain private in such a moment. And maybe no one spotted him, Zacchaeus the tax collector, up there in his sycamore tree. Or maybe they did, and laughed and pointed, until the whole crowd caught on and joined in the mirth, and one episode of tree climbing had turned into a public spectacle: Jericho's least favorite son and lackey of Romans, *treed.*

Jesus didn't laugh, though. He peered up through the branches at the man peering down at him and told Zacchaeus to come down. "Besides," Jesus added, cheerfully, "you've got dinner plans, Zacchaeus. I'm coming to your house, and salvation is too."

Zacchaeus had a change of heart that day, and, to be blunt, it was long overdue. He promised to amend his life and repay his neighbors for all he'd defrauded them, which was considerable. We could rejoice at that and call it a day. After all, it's his story; if the man wants to spend it up a tree, let him. Unless this isn't so much a story as an invitation, and we're supposed to join him up there. Maybe *up a tree* with Zacchaeus is exactly where we need to be right now or need to be willing to go.

As people of faith, we spend our lives trying to see Jesus: in Scripture, in the world, in the people we live and work alongside. Trying to see Jesus, just like Zacchaeus. And like him, we have to work for it, because Jesus is always on the move, passing through Jericho and the towns where we live and the stories we read in Scripture. We

Group Discussion Guide

Icebreakers: ABC Questions

1. Go around the circle and name something or someone from Scripture for each letter of the alphabet—the first person doing *A,* the second doing *B,* and so forth (without looking at the table of contents, of course!). You can do this with names, places, images, verbs, or anything else you can think of, as long as each person can point to a story where the word is featured.

2. If your group is multilingual, try the same icebreaker, with each person speaking in the language of their choice. Go around the circle, naming something or someone from Scripture in your chosen language, translating for one another as needed.

3. For a more challenging and competitive version of this game, have each person write down their own alphabetical list of biblical names, places, or images. Then share the lists, one letter at a time, earning one point for each word that no one else used. (For example, if your *I* is for Issachar and everyone else writes Israel, you get a point.)

4. Considering the author's choices for each letter, are there any letters of the alphabet for which you would have chosen an entirely different story? If your favorite biblical figure's initial was already taken, what other words or images related to their story could match them to different letters of the alphabet?

Questions for Discussing Individual Chapters

1. Was this story familiar to you? If so, can you remember how and when you first heard it and how you responded to it at the time? What did you notice this time that you hadn't noticed before? If it was not familiar to you, what details in the story stood out for you?

2. Do the characters in the story remind you of anyone you know? Do they help you see that person in a new light?

3. Are there questions you'd like to ask the characters in the story, to understand them and their situation better?

4. Has this story played out in your own life at some point, or in the lives of those around you? Is it a script you recognize?

5. If you could change one thing in the story to make it unfold differently, what would you change? Or if you could rewrite the ending, what would that rewrite be?

6. Is this a story—in full or edited form—that is important for children, youth, or young adults in your context to hear and discuss? How would you go about presenting it for each age group? What do you hope young people might learn from the story at different stages of their development?

7. Did this reflection prompt you to pull out a Bible and read more of the context around a story? Were there any surprises as you did?

8. Did this reflection interpret a story in a very different way than you had previously thought or heard? Share one or two ideas you had while reading this reflection that gave you a new insight into the story or characters.

Questions for Discussing the Book as a Whole

1. Choose a reflection that particularly spoke to you or had an impact on you in some way. Share why it is memorable for you.

2. Choose a reflection that shed light on an aspect of your childhood or home life. How did the reflection do this, and how did you experience it?

3. Choose a reflection that speaks into a situation or issue in your faith community. How did the reflection do this? Is there practical wisdom you can learn here about how your faith community might engage this situation or issue? How might you help to start that conversation?

4. Were there any reflections that challenged or unsettled you? Are you thinking differently now? What do you want to keep exploring?

5. Did you detect recurring themes in the book? How did the stories relate to one another?

6. Share one or two things you've learned about interpreting Scripture from your experience of reading the book. Were any of these new or surprising, challenging or liberating? Moving forward, is there anything you want to do differently in your own reading of Scripture? Are there any new interpretive practices you want to try?

Index of Scripture

221

Printed in the USA
CPSIA information can be obtained
at www.ICGtesting.com
LVHW011915170724
785385LV00006B/41